MAURICE WILES

Christian Theology and Inter-religious Dialogue

D1606395

SCM PRESS
London

TRINITY PRESS INTERNATIONAL
Philadelphia

First published 1992

SCM Press
26–30 Tottenham Road,
London N1 4BZ

Trinity Press International
3725 Chestnut Street,
Philadelphia Pa. 19104

British Library Cataloguing in Publication Data

Wiles, Maurice
   Christian Theology and Inter-religious
   Dialogue
   I. Title
   261.2

ISBN 0 334 02523 0

Library of Congress Cataloging-in-Publication Data

Wiles, Maurice F.
Christian theology and inter-religious dialogue/ Maurice Wiles.
            p.   cm.
   Includes bibliographical referenes and index.
         ISBN 1–56338–036–6
   1. Christianity and other religions. 2. Rahner, 1904– ,
I. Title.
BR127.W45   1992
261.2–dc20
                                             91–46556
                                                 CIP

Printed and bound in Great Britain by Mackays of Chatham PLC, Chatham, Kent

Contents

Preface

This is not a book that I expected to write. I did not doubt the importance of its theme, but the appropriateness of my experience for dealing with it. The responsibility for overcoming those reservations is mine, but various friends and circumstances have contributed to the emergence of the book. John Hick and Wilfred Cantwell Smith have ensured, both by their example and their counsel over the years, that the possibility of writing on this topic was never wholly discounted. Leslie Houlden heard an informal paper of mine on the subject to a society in Oxford and encouraged me to publish it in *Theology*.[1] An invitation to give the Ferguson Lectures in the University of Manchester in February 1991 provided the stimulus to develop my reflections more fully, with the earlier article serving as a preliminary sketch plan for the more extended argument of the lectures. David Pailin was a splendid host on that occasion, arranging opportunities for discussion with a variety of groups, offering lively theological comments of his own and, with Gwyneth, the generous hospitality of his home. A further invitation to give the Taylor lectures at Yale Divinity School enabled me to use some of the same material in a slightly different form with a different audience. I am very grateful to both these institutions for the honour of being asked to give lectures, and for the stimulus that has provided. In preparing the

lectures I have benefited greatly from discussion with Alan
Race, who also read an earlier draft of them and made
many helpful suggestions. I am grateful to all these friends,
and others, who have contributed to the coming to birth
of this book. I hope they won't be too disappointed with
the outcome.

Maurice Wiles

I

The Precedents of the Past

Few people can have less claim than I have to write on this subject. For I come to it as a Christian theologian who for the last twenty years has taught in a Theology Faculty which contains no positions directly committed to the study or teaching of any religious tradition other than the Christian. Nor have I myself had much direct experience of the kind of dialogue indicated by my title. I can claim, therefore, neither academic nor personal experience as justification for the task that I am undertaking. Yet in venturing to address the issue, I do not see myself as stepping aside from the main concerns of my work as a Christian theologian. For it is precisely that work which has forced me to take this question with increasing seriousness in recent years. The task of a Christian theologian, as I understand it, is to make sense of his or her Christian tradition in the light of our contemporary experience of the world in which we live. And if that is a proper understanding of the theologian's role, it requires him or her to pay serious attention to a variety of aspects of the contemporary world, even though it is impossible that he or she be expert in all of them. I have no scientific training, but one cannot speak appropriately about the doctrine of creation without some understanding of the picture of the physical world that modern science has opened up to us. In a similar way the question of inter-religious dialogue is an inescapable one for the theologian, however limited his or her personal experience of it, since the close co-existence of different faith communities in our one world – indeed for very many people the co-existence of such communities in the immediate locality or institution in which they live or work – is a distinctive feature of our experience.

One further word of warning about the validity of my limited credentials for this undertaking needs also to be made at the outset. Any expectations I might have had that expertise as a Christian *theologian* would automatically ensure that one has a significant contribution to make to inter-religious dialogue was rudely shattered on the one occasion in which I have taken part in a formal dialogue of that kind. Representatives of different faiths had gathered at Lambeth Palace to discuss a paper by John Taylor on 'The Theological Basis of Interfaith Dialogue'.[1] In the course of the meeting, a Jewish participant complained that the subject-matter of the discussion, as reflected by the title of John Taylor's paper, was itself not a neutral one but was already firmly slanted in a Christian direction. As a Jew, such dialogue did not for him need any theological basis. Only once, he declared, had he seen theology make a constructive contribution to inter-religious dialogue. It was a conference of Jews, Christians, and Muslims shortly after the Yom Kippur war. Naturally enough the meeting was a difficult one, and mutual suspicion was very much in evidence – until at one point Protestants and Catholics within the Christian delegation fell into dispute among themselves on some matter of theology. To both Jew and Muslim the point at issue seemed so abstruse, not to say absurd, that they began (for the first time) to look at each other in shared incredulity, which grew into shared smiles and shared laughter. From that point on, the conference went splendidly. Such was the nature of the only positive contribution of theology to inter-religious understanding that he had experienced.

It was a sobering story for a Christian theologian. The role of theology for the development of inter-religious understanding may indeed be limited, because theology may have a very different role to play in different religions (even assuming that it has *some* role in each of them). But whatever the particular problems that people of other religions may have to face before they can enter fruitfully into dialogue with Christians, it seems clear that for Christians who want to embark on dialogue with people of other religious traditions in a way which is consistent with the integrity of their own Christian profession, there is need to reflect about the theological basis on which they are doing so. Many Christians today are acutely aware of the need for a changed and more constructive relation between the world's religions. They may have been brought to this awareness by a new respect for some other religious tradition, engendered either by the perceived piety of their neighbours or by the reading of that religion's spiritual classics. In other cases their concern may have been brought about more by fear at the prospect of ever increasing religious conflict in the absence of any improvement in mutual understanding. But whatever the motives of their desire for improved understanding, they are often held back from the idea of dialogue by feelings of guilt; genuine dialogue with another religious tradition, it seems to them, would necessarily involve disloyalty to their own fundamental Christian commitment. And while the Lord may save by love or fear, he does not save by misplaced guilt. So if, as I believe, that guilt is misplaced, it needs to be exorcised. And that is an essentially theological task. That, therefore, is the relatively limited, but nonetheless important, task that I have set myself. In terms of a useful distinction drawn by Michael Barnes, what I shall be concerned with is not a theology *of* dialogue, that is to say 'a theology which emerges directly from the inter-religious encounter'; it is rather a theology *for* dialogue, one 'which prepares for that encounter'.[2] I shall not, that is to say, be asking what Christian theology might have to learn from Hinduism or Islam. Any worthwhile answer to that question can only be the outcome of a sustained, empathetic engagement with another religious tradition, of which I have no personal experience. I shall rather be asking: what are the implications for Christianity of acknowledging that some other religion may be a proper partner in open dialogue?

The answer to that question depends on what is implied by the phrase 'open dialogue'. There is a minimal sense in which the word 'dialogue' indicates no more than the basic courtesy of allowing the other person to speak, even though one is convinced that he or she is wholly mistaken and that one has nothing to learn from what he or she may say. But in speaking of inter-religious or interfaith dialogue, something more than that is implied. Dialogue in that context is not just the name for a more civilized or socially acceptable way of achieving the same ends that were previously intended by the one-sided preaching to the unconverted. It involves a genuinely reciprocal process, in which the two parties stand on an equal footing of readiness to receive as well as to give. And if that is what is implied by 'dialogue', it necessarily involves seeing the other religion as in some sense a revelation of God from which we need to learn. That, in its turn, poses the question: can Christian theology develop a doctrine of other religions which sees religions other than itself as also falling within the economy of God in such a way that a

Christian can with full propriety enter into dialogue with them in the expectation of receiving as well as offering truth from God? That question, indeed, is an inescapable one for any Christian who has abandoned the view that other religious traditions are to be seen exclusively as manifestations of the demonic or of human pride, whether he or she participates directly in dialogue or not. As Wilfred Cantwell Smith wrote thirty years ago:

> From now on any serious intellectual statement of the Christian faith must include, if it is to serve its purpose among men, some sort of doctrine of other religions. We explain the fact that the Milky Way is there by the doctrine of creation, but how do we explain that the *Bhagavad Gita* is there?[3]

The deep-seated Christian hesitation about the compatibility of Christian commitment and open dialogue with other religions is to be found in a variety of forms. It may base itself on key texts of scripture. Geoffrey Parrinder comments that any exposition of another religion to a Western audience is

> liable to be challenged with biblical texts such as 'there is no other name under heaven given among men by which we must be saved' (Acts 4.12) or 'no one comes to the Father but my me' (John 14.6).[4]

Alternatively the objection may take a broader form, the suggested dialogue being seen more generally as a desertion of the way in which the church has understood its faith down the ages. More explicitly, and more fundamentally, it is likely to be regarded as conflicting with the absolute claims of Christianity, particularly in relation to the person and work of Christ.

How well-founded are such feelings? There is a natural tendency among those who share my desire to overcome such attitudes, to deny that they have any secure grounding in scripture or tradition. John Macquarrie speaks of such people as

> deluded by the particularly reprehensible superstition that their religion is superior to all others and that the particular revelation of God which they believe to have been vouchsafed to them is the touchstone and norm by which all other revelations whatsoever must be judged,

and goes on to claim that such ideas

> have no foundation in any reasonable interpretation of the Christian faith as it has come to down to us in the scriptures and in the best traditions of the Church.[5]

Much as I might wish that it were so, that seems to me to claim too much. I do not find myself able to deny that the approach to inter-religious dialogue that I shall be commending does involve a substantial change in what has characteristically been the dominant self-understanding of Christianity and of the church down the ages. Nevertheless I shall still be making the lesser claim that it does not represent a sheer bouleversement of past attitudes, unable to lay claim to any precedents in the earlier teaching and practice of the church. That is the issue I will be considering in the remainder of this chapter. In the next chapter I shall argue that the church has been faced for some time with a series of other pressures, arising out of other changes in contemporary knowledge and experience of the world, which are not directly connected with the question of a plurality of faiths but which call for the same sort of modification in our traditional theological understanding as a whole. The question of a change in our relation to other religious traditions is not, therefore, something that arises on its own to challenge an otherwise unchanging theological tradition. It is, rather, part of a much wider phenomenon of change. In the third chapter I shall look at the way in which one recent Christian theologian, Karl Rahner, has tried to incorporate these changes into a coherent theological position, to see how far his theology provides an appropriate theological framework for inter-religious dialogue. And in the final chapter I shall seek to build on Rahner's approach and offer my own account of a Christian theology for dialogue.

I propose to begin, therefore, by considering the objection that the invitation to an open dialogue with other religions, with a view to finding as well as communicating truth, represents a radical reversal of the teaching of scripture and that of the main body of the church down the ages. I do not intend to discuss at length the evidence of scripture, though the issue will recur indirectly throughout the argument of the chapter as a whole. But a brief discussion of the two much quoted texts, to which Geoffrey Parrinder alludes, may serve to illustrate the two approaches to the evidence of the past to which I have already drawn attention – the one anxious to emphasize continuity, the other laying its stress on the difference between what was said and done in the past and what has to be said and done now. Some people affirm that any appeal to those texts as grounds for holding back from inter-religious dialogue involves a misunderstanding of them through failure to pay attention to their proper context. The declaration that 'there is no other name under

heaven given among men whereby we must be saved'
comes from the Acts of the Apostles and is part of Peter's
explanation to the Jewish leaders when challenged about
his healing of the blind man at the gate Beautiful. The
'salvation' of which it speaks is, they insist, the 'healing'
of the lame man, which is the issue in dispute. The same
word in Greek covers both meanings, and the affirmation,
they argue, cannot legitimately be extended to the wider
context of whether or not salvation is accessible through
other religions.[6] And the statement that 'no one comes to
the Father but by me' comes from the Fourth Gospel and
is therefore to be seen as spoken by the Logos incarnate.
Like other statements in the same gospel (such as 'Before
Abraham was I am'), it is to be understood as referring
to the Logos, the light who enlightens everyone, rather
than to Jesus, the first-century historical figure. So understood it is not in conflict with the possibility that the Logos
may be leading people to the Father in and through other
religions.[7] Those are valid considerations in relation to the
significance of the two texts. But they do not rule out
altogether any possible significance of those texts for our
present concerns. The potential meaning of texts is not
necessarily restricted to authorial intention or to the significance apprehensible by their original readership. Moreover, even if it may indeed be true that their original
context is too restricted to justify the radically negative
attitude to the saving potential of all other religious traditions that is so regularly ascribed to them, they are not
quite as innocent on that score as we have been implying
so far. There is no denying that part of their original
context is the anti-Jewish polemic of Luke's Gospel and
the Acts of the Apostles in the one case and of John's
Gospel in the other.[8] They do involve a deliberately negative attitude to the Judaism of their day, from which we

may well need to distance ourselves in any contemporary dialogue.

When we turn on to the later teaching of the church, the negativity of the dominant tradition is even more pronounced. I will take just two examples, one Catholic and one Protestant. In the fifteenth century the Council of Florence affirmed that

> no one outside the Catholic church, not only pagans but also Jews and heretics and schismatics, can share in eternal life, but will perish in the eternal fire prepared for the devil and his angels.[9]

A hundred years later, Luther wrote in strikingly similar terms:

> Those who are outside Christianity, be they heathens, Turks, Jews or even false Christians and hypocrites . . . cannot expect either love or any blessing from God, and accordingly remain in eternal wrath and perdition.[10]

The precise delineation of the sphere within which one needs to be, in order to be a recipient of salvation, is significantly different in the two cases, but the verdict on all who belong to any other religious tradition than the Christian, properly defined, is unhesitatingly the same. This austere doctrine was, admittedly, subject to qualification and modification. The principle of the 'baptism of desire', for example, allowed that those with no knowledge of Christianity who followed their conscience and lived morally could be deemed to have desired baptism and thereby to have come within the saving fold of the Christian church. But even that concession did not involve any positive evaluation of the religion to which such a person might belong. It was the natural law of God written in their hearts which was the medium of such abnormal occasions of salvation. The concession did not involve attributing any positive role to any other religious tradition.

Admittedly there were other strands of Christian teaching. Those who seek to stress a line of continuity between contemporary desire for dialogue and earlier tradition look particularly to the teaching of the second-century apologists, especially Justin Martyr's ascription of the wisdom of Heraclitus and Socrates to their participation in the same divine Logos that was incarnate in Jesus. And when John Macquarrie spoke of 'the best traditions of the church' as being at odds with the assertion of the superiority of Christianity over all other religions, what he had particularly in mind was the broadly catholic view which has been prepared to recognize a genuine, if very limited, knowledge of God in other religions. But while there certainly are strands of teaching to be found that are significantly different from the denunciations characteristic of the dominant tradition, they still fall a long way short of providing a basis for that open dialogue with other religions being proposed today. The nearest we come to that is, perhaps, the fascinating figure of Nicholas of Cusa, a fifteenth-century cardinal, who tells of 'a vision, in which he saw how the differences of the warring sects were permanently reconciled in a vast system of religious unity'. In that vision, 'pagan and Christian are jumbled up in a remarkable order' as there appear 'a Greek, an Italian, a Hindu, an Arab, a Chaldean, a Jew, a Scythian, a Persian, a Syrian, a Spaniard, a Tartar, a German, a Bohemian and finally an Englishman'. For Nicholas 'each system possesses a certain degree of truth' and 'only through a study of the various systems can one have an inkling of the "unity of the unattainable truth" '.[11]

But Nicholas is an exception. The dominant tradition with which Catholics particularly have to come to terms if they are to embark on dialogue is the old insistence that 'outside the Church there is no salvation' (*extra ecclesiam nulla salus*). And once again we find a range of strategies brought to bear between those who want to stress a strong element of continuity and those who are ready to acknowledge the sharpness of the break with the past. Some claim that the word 'church' in the formula does not refer to the visible, historical church, but to the mystical body of Christ and therefore does not conflict with the affirmation of salvation in and through other religions.[12] It is perfectly true that the original context of the saying was the issue of schism and heresy and not that of other religions. The phrase derives from Cyprian (*Ep.* 73.21) writing about the invalidity of baptism administered by heretical groups. It is not, therefore, in its original authorial intention a saying specifically designed to deny the possibility of salvation through the medium of some quite other religious tradition. But the intended reference of the word 'church' was unquestionably the visible, historical church. The continuity that is secured by maintaining the same words and changing the significance of the word 'church' is specious. Raimundo Panikkar offers an extreme, but refreshingly explicit, form of this approach. 'My interpretation', he writes, 'is to turn it around and affirm that the statement means that the Church is the locus of salvation, wherever this place may be and however it may appear'.[13] Such an inversion of the saying comes much closer to a reversal than to a refurbishment of its meaning. Hans Küng is right to protest against such 'pseudo-orthodox stretching of the meaning of Christian concepts like "church" '. It is, as he says, 'no answer to the challenge of religions' and it fails to do justice to the 'epoch-making reversal of the attitude to those outside the "holy Roman Church"' enacted at the second Vatican Council.[14] Paul Knitter seeks to find a middle road of evaluation, when he describes the second Vatican Council's *Declaration on the Relationship of the Church to Non-Christian Religions* as 'a watershed' and goes on to say that 'it carries on the tradition, but does so in clearly new directions'.[15] But the change of direction is, in my view, much closer to a U-turn than to a minor deviation. The attempt to trace links with some aspects of earlier tradition must not be allowed to play down the radical nature of the change that has already taken place.

So far I have been considering how far the attitude of the church to other religions through the centuries acts as a genuine disincentive to inter-religious dialogue. And I have argued that for anyone who understands Christian faithfulness in terms of continuing the old traditions more or less unchanged it will inevitably be experienced as a strong disincentive, even if there is just enough variety in that tradition for it to fall short of constituting an absolute veto. The positive case for dialogue will have to rest on a different perception of the way to faith, which points to a form of Christian faithfulness compatible with radical change. The development of such a case will be the aim of the next chapter. But before we move on to those considerations, it needs to be remembered that there are other ways of reflecting on past tradition in addition to recounting that tradition's explicit affirmations about the status of other religions. Every tradition is more than the sum of its public declarations. Three other ways of assessing our Christian past, which may serve to moderate any sense of its monolithic opposition to an open dialogue with other religions, deserve to be considered.

An important element in what I have called the deep-seated Christian hesitation about inter-religious dialogue is the fear that it is inconsistent with other indispensable Christian beliefs. The evident presupposition of that fear is that Christian beliefs should be consistent with one another. Otherwise inconsistency would not constitute a barrier to the holding of particular beliefs. So if traditional Christian attitudes are rightly to exercise a restraining influence for that kind of reason, it is essential that they should themselves constitute a coherent whole; an inconsistent set of beliefs cannot be used to rule out adoption of some new belief on the ground that it would be inconsistent with those already existing beliefs. It is necessary, therefore, to ask whether the old tradition on this issue itself stands up to the test of consistency. Christian faith insists that God is a god of universal love and yet, on any strict interpretation of the principle of no salvation outside the church or outside Christianity, God is understood to be denying to the majority of humankind any possibility of salvation. John Hick has given considerable weight to this argument. He describes how he himself once held that view, but how, because his attention was concentrated on the recipients of God's grace rather than on those to whom all access to it was denied, he remained unaware of its internal inconsistency.[16] His argument has been criticized as 'rationalistic',[17] but that criticism must be firmly rejected. A concern for consistency, especially moral consistency, in our affirmations about God cannot be dismissed as a form of false rationalism; it is fundamental, and without it there is no possibility of a responsible Christian theology. It is true, as Hick himself acknowledges, that the qualifications to the principle of no salvation outside the church, to which I have already referred, were designed expressly to meet that objection. But I think he is right to regard them as unsatisfactory *ad hoc* modifications, which fall a long way short of achieving their intention, and to suggest that they are better seen as pointers to the need for some more radical 'reversal' or 'repeal' of the older view, of the kind that some commentators have seen enacted at the second Vatican Council.[18]

Essentially the same challenge to the moral consistency of the tradition can be put in another way. I Timothy 2.4 speaks of God as desiring 'all men to be saved and to come to a knowledge of the truth'. Yet most of the outstanding theologians of the church's history, Augustine and Aquinas among its classic exponents, and Bucer and Calvin at the time of the Reformation, have gone to great pains to insist that that text must not be taken at its face value. Various more qualified interpretations have been proposed. It refers only to the predestined, or, say others, to representatives of all classes of humankind, rather than to all individual men and women. The one thing it must not be allowed to mean is 'that there is no one whose salvation [God] does not desire'.[19] Over against that central tradition of Christian exegesis, we may set the premise with which Karl Rahner in this century has approached the question of Christianity and the non-Christian religions. 'If we wish to be Christians', he says, 'we must profess belief in the universal and serious salvific purpose of God towards all men which is true even within the post-paradisean phase of salvation dominated by original sin'.[20] In other words, the text is to be taken at its face value and not applied to some theoretical desire of God, no longer valid in this sinful world. Which account is to be regarded as more consistent with the basic Christian belief in the universal love of God? In the face of that question, I find it impossible to assert that the dominant Christian tradition has shown such internal consistency that a radically revised understanding of other religions can be ruled out *a priori* as liable to disrupt an otherwise fully coherent system of belief.

Christian tradition, as has already been pointed out, is not only a matter of the official beliefs and expressed teachings of the church; it is a matter also of its history and practices. That fact indicates a second supplementary way of reflecting on the significance of past tradition. At first sight, the historical record of the church's past will appear rather to exacerbate than to qualify the negativity of its formal statements in relation to other religions. The treatment accorded to Jews throughout Christendom and the story of the Crusades show the hostile evaluation of Jews and Muslims finding full expression in the brutalities of Christianly motivated practice. And while some of that practice may be ascribed to a failure to live up to the acknowledged tenets of belief (a characteristic that applies to all religions), quite a lot of it was explicitly encouraged and authorized on the basis of Christian beliefs. The dominant tenor of Christian practice tells the same story as the dominant strain in Christian teaching, and is substantially dependent upon it.

But there is another, less conscious, side to the history of Christian faith, which tells a rather different story. Like other religious traditions, Christianity is not a static entity. It has developed over the centuries. Despite its strong and consistent repudiation of the beliefs of all other religions, that process of development has involved more by way of syncretistic incorporation of aspects of other religious traditions than Christians have usually been prepared to acknowledge. This is particularly evident in the early formative years of the emergence of the Christian church as the dominant religious power in the Roman world. The church showed costly courage in maintaining its distinct identity over against the other religions of the empire. Yet there was also a process of assimilation that operated at a variety of levels, particularly in the development of Christian festivals and in forms of Christian piety. It is usually the blood of the martyrs, resulting from their refusal to allow any compromise with other forms of religious practice, to which the triumph of the church is ascribed. But Arnold Toynbee suggests that there is also another side to the story. He describes it as one of the conditions for Christianity's emergence as the victor among the religions of the Roman Empire 'that it should and did absorb into itself what was valuable in those other religions'.[21]

But perhaps the best example is the positive contribution of the Hellenistic philosophico-religious tradition to the development of normative Christian doctrine in those first centuries of the church's history. Even those who acknowledge and approve the contribution of Hellenism to Christian thought tend to speak of it as if it were a purely intellectual or philosophical process. I have deliberately described it as a philosophico-*religious* tradition. For the Platonism of the early Christian era was no mere school philosophy; it was a religious phenomenon, and its impact was religious as well as intellectual. The point is perhaps clearest if we start with the example of Philo, the first-century Jewish writer of Alexandria. Philo's Hellenism did not only affect his thought. Nor, of course, did it stop him being a Jew, but it radically affected the kind of Jew he was religiously. Christian scholars, for whom Philo has been an important focus of study, have perhaps been able to see this to be so in his case more readily than they have been able to see it in the case of the early Christian Fathers. Yet they were involved in the same process. The division between orthodoxy and heresy in the early church was not a division between those who kept their Christianity pure and those who compromised it with alien elements from another faith, however much the orthodox may have liked to present it in those terms; it was between different ways of bringing together their Christian inheritance with the religious insights of the Platonic tradition. And those insights contributed positively to the emergent religion of the triumphant orthodoxy. The Christianity of the early Fathers, of for example a Gregory of Nyssa or a Dionysius the Areopagite, was affected at its heart by things learnt from a distinct religious tradition, one that had developed outside the stream of Jewish and Christian history. And many of those things learnt in that way are a part of the Christianity that we know today.

Of course the practice and the ideas that were taken over were not taken over unchanged. They were transformed by being brought into a new, Christian context. But that is not to deny their substantial influence on the Christianity into which they had been introduced. The Christian context into which they came was itself transformed by their incorporation. The fact that Christianity has drawn on other religious traditions to the extent that it has in the course of its historical development poses a question-mark against Christianity's own negative evaluation of those religious traditions from which it has drawn so fruitfully. Looking at the history of the Christian tradition in this way, it can be understood to reveal implicitly the possibility of a more favourable evaluation of other religions than it has ever allowed itself to give voice to explicitly. Here, it may be claimed, is yet another way in which past tradition, despite its predominantly negative character, may also be seen as encouraging the possibility of a changed attitude to other religions and not simply militating against it.

Finally, we need to recall one other feature central to the character of Christian faith, which should prepare us for the acceptability of radical change within a continuity of Christian faith and practice. One of the hallmarks of Christianity is that it is a prophetic religion. In other words it is a religion with the right, or rather the duty of protest against its own currently established form, written into it. A prophetic book like that of Jonah represents a protest against the narrow outlook of the Jewish leadership of the time. The teaching of Jesus embodied a similar protest, challenging, for example, the contemporary understanding of the Torah's pronouncements about divorce in the light of a wider appeal to God's creative purpose. The Christian movement itself began its life with a similar conflict about the propriety of opening its doors freely to Gentiles as well as Jews. And although we speak of the 'development' of Christianity from that time to this, the process has never been a matter of smooth progression. It has regularly been punctuated, and not only at the Reformation, by similar movements of protest, giving rise at times to quite radical changes of direction.

The examples that I have chosen as illustrations of the prophetic character of Christianity have all been ones in which the prophet has challenged a narrower conception of God's purpose in the light of a wider vision. And that, of course, has been deliberate; it is consonant with the proposal for a move towards a more open dialogue that I am concerned to commend. But prophecy has not always taken that form. It has often stood for a stricter interpretation of God's will against what has seemed to it too open and too lax an understanding. Those who feel that the present tentative moves towards inter-religious dialogue are a dangerous dilution of true faith can appeal to prophetic precedent as justification for their protests, as legitimately as can those who advocate a more radical change in that direction. The recollection of the prophetic character of Christian faith is not designed to prove that the move towards an open inter-religious dialogue is thereby shown to be justified. It is designed only to support the preliminary thesis that radical change of the kind envisaged cannot be ruled out as inadmissible in advance. The more positive case remains to be put in the succeeding chapters.

2

The Pressures of the Present

In the previous chapter, I acknowledged that the main Christian tradition was clearly opposed to any positive evaluation of other religions and that it was therefore neither improper nor unnatural for a Christian to feel serious hesitation about entering into open dialogue with members of other religious traditions. But I argued that there were aspects of that older Christian tradition which made it inappropriate to rule out such dialogue as an impossibility for Christians. I want now to develop some wider arguments that will suggest that the moves already being made in that direction ought to be regarded as not merely allowable for Christians, but actually incumbent on them. But before doing so I propose to deal with one line of reasoning, which would dismiss any such argument as irrelevant rationalization of a phenomenon which is wholly explicable in other terms.

Some sociologists of religion have seen the earlier emergence of an ecumenical movement between previously hostile Christian denominations as a reaction to Christianity's loss of prestige and plausibility in an age of secularism. The move towards inter-religious dialogue readily lends itself to be understood in the same way. The parallel between the ecumenical movement and the move towards inter-religious dialogue is certainly a valid one. For the ecumenical movement, particularly as it relates to catholic-protestant rapprochement, had to overcome precisely the same sort of theoretically based exclusivism and denunciation that has characterized the relation between Christianity and other religions. In catholic eyes, protestants, every bit as much as Jews and Muslims, were among those who were outside the church and for whom therefore there was no salvation. And for many protestants, Roman Catholics were not merely in error, but were seen, either in general or in the person of the Pope, as the embodiment of anti-Christ. In the ecumenical case, as well as in the inter-religious case, the perception of the gulf was of one that could not be overcome without the sacrifice of divinely given and inalienable truth. And the sociologists' account of the motives leading to the partial overcoming of those unbridgeable gulfs is undoubtedly a part of the story. Christians ought not to deny its validity, unless it claims to be providing a total explanation of those changes. Indeed it is particularly important that Christians do recognize the substantial element of truth in that account. Otherwise they may be unreasonably surprised or offended when people of other religious traditions stop before accepting any invitation to dialogue and ask why Christians did not show such enthusiasm for dialogue in the so-called ages of faith, which were also ages of Christian supremacy.

But although that is undoubtedly part of the story, it is certainly not the whole story. It is true of all forms of social and political change that they are seldom realized in practice without the pressure of some external force or circumstance. But there must also be the potential for change, inherent in the society or the body politic. And it is the same with religious change. Whatever external forces helped give rise to the ecumenical movement, that movement was also the outcome of a changed understanding of how Christian truth comes to be known. Truth, as well as expediency, has had a part to play. Modifications to the absolutist claims which protestants and catholics alike have very often made for (as it now seems) their particular version of Christian faith are the result not only of a loss of nerve, or a loss of concern for truth, but also of a very genuine concern for truth. That same mixture of motives, arising out of external pressures and internal convictions, was operative in the case of our more distant forebears in the faith also. The difference between us lies not in differing degrees of concern for truth, but in a changed understanding of the nature of the evidence on which it now seems proper for us to draw and the way in which we believe our concern for truth has to be worked out in practice.

In this chapter, therefore, my aim will be to reflect on the nature of that changed understanding of how Christian truth comes to be known and to draw out some of its implications for the possibility of inter-religious dialogue. It is a basically familiar, but highly complex story, and I shall order my reflections under the three headings of the appeal to experience, the nature of religious language, and the changing character of religions as historical phenomena.

First then the apprehension of Christian truth always involves a process of interpretation. It cannot simply be read off from authoritative texts or declared by an infallible magisterium. Indeed the scriptural texts themselves, which have so often been used in that kind of directly authoritative way in the past, can readily be seen to embody an understanding of the world, that is in part the product of the culturally conditioned outlook, characteristic of the author's age and community. The more formal statements of Christian belief in the later life of the church have taken shape from the interplay of those texts and the changing patterns of experience through which the Christian church has passed. And finally there is no access for us now to Christian truth from scripture or from the church's affirmations of its faith, which does not go through the interpretative prism of our own personal and communal experience. That is not to deny the role of scripture as a medium of divine revelation. But it is to insist that just as any knowledge of God through the created order is dependent on the manner of our apprehension and interpretation of it, so there is also a similar indirectness about the scriptural revelation. The form in which it comes to us is inextricably bound up with the particular experiences and understandings of the world that characterized the scriptural authors and their communities. And what we learn from scripture now is similarly dependent on our restricted range of experience and understanding. What is being affirmed here in relation to Christian truth is part of a wider phenomenon that applies to human knowledge as a whole. There is a subjective element in all human knowing which influences the content of what is known as well as the manner in which that content is apprehended.

It is important to safeguard against possible misunderstandings of this stress on the subjective and interpretative character of religious knowing. It does not imply that religious knowledge is simply our personal interpretation of our own individual present experiences. We stand in a tradition, and the particular forms of experience that are open to us and that we enjoy are in large measure dependent on that tradition. Religious knowledge is not being turned into a purely private affair; it is a public and social form of knowledge. Nor does it imply that such knowledge cannot embody a valid apprehension of some transcendent divine reality. But the form of that apprehension, like the types of experience through which it is apprehended, is ineluctably controlled by the particular tradition in which we stand.

This way of understanding the road to Christian truth has both contributed to the rise of the ecumenical movement and been reinforced by it. If experience, embodied in and shaped by a particular tradition of language, culture and practical life, plays so crucial a role in the apprehension of Christian truth, the question is inevitably raised: whose experience and what traditions do we need to take account of? Once catholics or protestants have accepted that there *is* salvation and a knowledge of God outside the church, even if only in the sense of outside their own ecclesiastical tradition, it becomes impossible to justify ignoring that wider range of tradition and experience in one's concern for Christian truth. It may not be evident at once how the differing teachings of the differing Christian traditions – about the sacraments, for example – or the differing patterns of experience that have been built up over the centuries of relative isolation, are to be shared and allowed to influence the theological understanding of each community. That is something that can only be worked out gradually, and genuine dialogue between people, with a readiness not only to communicate to the other but also oneself to be changed by the other, is an essential element in the process. That a process of that kind is a necessary element in any serious search for Christian truth is now widely accepted. What would have been anathema to our forebears in both communities is now virtually taken for granted. The degree to which the older traditions of competing theological understanding will remain clearly distinct in the long run, so that people will continue to speak of Catholic, Lutheran and Reformed understandings of Christian truth, remains an open question. What is more important and what, I believe, can be affirmed with full confidence is that the process of mutual learning of the kind on which Christians have embarked in the ecumenical movement helps each communion to correct distortions of the truth that have arisen in the past as a result of the more restricted range of their earlier separated traditions. It leads to an enrichment, not an impoverishment of those traditions.

This very general account of how Christian belief is built up and finds appropriate expression would, I think, meet with broad agreement within the scholarly world – provided the concept of 'experience' is not understood to refer only to private states of feeling, but that its integral relation to the language, culture and practical life of a community is fully recognized. Keith Ward, for example, in his book *The Living God* gives a basically similar account of revelation in terms of the interpretation of experience in a living tradition with the aid of reflection, prayerful attention and inspired teaching or writing. His concern in that book is specifically with Christian faith, but towards the end of his chapter on revelation, he writes:

> There are, of course, a number of great religious traditions in the world. In general, the account of revelation I have given here would apply to them too, though naturally there would be differences of emphasis and analysis of the human situation and its destiny.[1]

That recognition of an apparent similarity of pattern in the form of Christian revelation and that which is characteristic of other religious traditions inescapably poses the further questions: Ought we to be taking account of their experience also in that approach to truth which characterizes the ecumenical movement? Are we right to restrict those who are properly to be involved to other *Christian* communions? In the case of the intra-Christian ecumenical movement, we have abandoned earlier attitudes to those other communions as enemies of the truth and have learnt to see them as necessary partners in our quest for truth. And we have done so because we recognize that for all of us a restriction of the range of human experience and interpretations on which we draw to that which is to be found specifically within our own particular Christian confession, runs the risk of narrowing and distorting our grasp of truth. On what grounds then can we exclude the experience of others who stand in another religious tradition, apparently characterized by a basically similar pattern of revelation? How can we know in advance that there may not be there a complementary apprehension of God from which we have much to learn? The case that I am making is put with telling simplicity by Hugo Meynell in an article commending 'a new dialectic of religions' as the most appropriate road in the search for religious truth. 'I may well' he writes,

> have a lively sense that my own beliefs are dependent merely on the evidence so far attended to, and the possibilities so far envisaged, by me and by my community. In studying the beliefs of those of other cultures than my own, and attending to the evidence, and the envisaged possibilities, on which these beliefs are based, I am very likely to come across something which I and my community have overlooked.[2]

Nevertheless, the assumption that since our concern is to find partners in the attempt to grasp *Christian* truth, it should be restricted to *Christian* bodies seems natural enough. But we have already recalled how natural it seemed to our forebears to restrict their concern in that task exclusively to catholic or protestant tradition. So the assumption that we restrict our concern to other Christian bodies, however natural it seems, calls for justification. And that justification is not as easily provided as might be expected. Precisely because of the universal claims that Christians want to make for Christ as the embodiment of the divine Logos, they cannot say that they are concerned with a truth that relates only to the sphere of the Christian church. I referred earlier to Wilfred Cantwell Smith's insistence that we need to relate the existence of the *Bhagavad Gita*, for example, to our Christian understanding of God's action in the world. But in the light of the analysis of the way to Christian truth that I have been outlining, it would seem to follow that it is not merely the existence of the *Bhagavad Gita* of which we will have to take account. We will also need to take account of the interpretation of God and the world that it presents and which has found expression in the lives of those who have sought to live in the light of its wisdom. We cannot, it would seem, rule out their experience and deny the potentiality of its having some contribution to make to our Christian apprehension of God, since that God is understood to be the one source 'from whom all thoughts of truth . . . proceed'.

Any justification of the restriction of our ecumenical approach to truth exclusively to other Christian bodies would have to be based on a claim that we can know in advance, on the basis of what we already know as Christians, that other religious traditions have no contribution to make towards any religiously significant or saving apprehension of truth about God. And that claim has indeed been a characteristic not only of extremist sects, but of one of the most distinguished forms of twentieth-century protestant theology. John Macquarrie cites Emil Brunner's words that 'a real Christian faith is impossible apart from the conviction that here and *here alone* is salvation' and comments bluntly that 'this is fanatical talk'. He finds it 'astonishing that in the middle of the twentieth century there should still be influential theologians clinging to the myth – for it is nothing more – of the unique, exclusive once-for-all revelation'.[3] I fully endorse Macquarrie's robust dismissal of Brunner's claim. But if that dismissal is to carry conviction, we need to see how it is that theologians, so fully conscious of the ambivalent character of the history of Christianity, could still find themselves able to make so sweeping a claim. Were they simply continuing the claim of Christianity to absolute superiority over all other religions that has been so prominent a feature of the Christian past? If pressed, Brunner has to acknowledge that there is a sense in which he is doing that, but his real rejoinder is that the form of the question is misconceived. Christian faith, he writes,

> cannot admit that its faith is one species of the genus 'religion', or if it does so, only in the sense in which it regards itself as the true religion in contrast to the other false religions.[4]

In other words, it is only in response to a question that has been wrongly put (one that treats Christianity as just one example of the general category 'religion') that a Christian might have to assert the truth of his or her religion over against the falsity of all others.

This claim that genuine Christian faith is not to be classified as a religion was carried through in an even more thorough-going way by Hendrick Kraemer and by Karl

Barth. They seek to avoid the implication that their attitude to other religions represents an arrogant affirmation
of the superiority and exclusive truth of their own religion
by allowing that their criticisms of religion apply to Christianity as well. All religions, including Christianity, are
essentially human constructions. As such they are forms
of human self-assertion over against God. 'The main thing
about all religions' says Kraemer, '– the heart and soul of
them so to speak – is that they are a *fleeing* from God';
they are 'in their ultimate and essential meaning and significance, *erroneous*'.[5] And over against that conception
of Christianity as a religion which hinders our apprehension of God, Kraemer sets Christ as '*the* Revelation of
God' who stands as judge over every religion. Barth works
out essentially the same antithesis with a more self-con-
sciously paradoxical use of the concept of religion. He
insists strongly that all religion is unbelief, and that that
implies that Christianity is unbelief. But he also affirms
that 'revelation singles out the Church as the *locus* of true
religion', and that where there is response to the promise
of that revelation, there is the 'grace of God, which, of
course, differentiates our religion, the Christian, from all
others as the true religion'.[6] Revelation negates all religion
as unbelief, and at the same time marks Christianity off
as the true religion.

Now Kraemer and Barth are quite right to insist that
Christianity as a religion needs continually to be criticized
in the light of Christ. That is a fundamental feature of the
prophetic principle to which I alluded towards the end of
the last chapter and which, I suggested, is a key reason for
expecting that a radical revision of our accepted attitude to
other religions may prove to be both possible and appropriate. The contrast they express by setting Christ over
against Christianity is an important one; it has served the

church well in encouraging particular acts of witness over against evil forms of contemporary culture, as in the Barmen declaration. But such acts of costly faithfulness are not dependent on and do not justify the absolute way in which that contrast is expressed. There is no Christ accessible to us in total independence of Christianity as a religion. There is no road to a knowledge of Jesus or of an original Christian gospel which does not come through the channels of human interpretation and critical evaluation. That to which we have access in our sources comes to us already embedded in a variety of particular and culturally specific forms. Kraemer and Barth are not only, in Macquarrie's words, 'clinging to the myth . . . of a unique, exclusive, once-for-all revelation'; they are asserting the availability of a revelation – or, more precisely, to use their own language, 'The Revelation' – which is independent of, and therefore able to stand in judgment over, every form of culture and of religion to be found anywhere in the world. Such an assertion stands against, and in my view is wholly unable to stand up to, the whole gamut of evidence as to how religious understanding has actually developed in relation to Christian faith or to any other form of faith. And Barth half acknowledges this when he speaks of revelation as singling out the church as the *locus* of true religion, thus differentiating 'our religion, the Christian, from all others as the true religion'. Despite some important insights that it has to offer, this whole approach is unable in the last analysis to escape the charge that it involves at its base a premature, and therefore unacceptable affirmation of the superiority of Christianity as the one true religion.

But there is another objection of a less theoretical and less absolute kind which may well be brought against the proposal for inter-religious dialogue as an ingredient in the Christian search for truth, parallel to the already tried ecumenical dialogue within Christianity. In the passage I quoted from Keith Ward, in which he stressed the similarity between accounts of revelation in Christianity and in other religious traditions, he ended with a qualifying clause: 'though naturally', the quotation ended, 'there would be differences of emphasis and analysis of the human situation and its destiny'. That, to put the point mildly, is surely something of an understatement. Even allowing that the nature of our access to religious knowing rules out any *a priori* affirmation of Christian revelation as the only locus of saving religious truth, does not, the sheer difference of fundamental understanding, let alone downright contradiction of particular beliefs, between the various religious traditions make the suggestion that inter-religious dialogue could be a contributory path to Christian truth really absurd? Such dialogue might indeed have a value in removing grounds for mutual suspicion and hostility that often arise through ignorance or misunder-standing of each other's traditions – and that is not a goal to be despised. But can it really contribute to each other's grasp of truth?

I want to consider a form of this objection from one who is not only firmly committed to inter-religious dialogue but also profoundly appreciative of the spiritual depths inherent in religious traditions other than the Christian. In the paper on 'The Theological Basis of Interfaith Dialogue' that I alluded to at the beginning of the first chapter, John Taylor brings out clearly what is bound to be a central issue for anyone who (like himself) has a deep commitment both to his or her own faith and to dialogue with others. In it he speaks of that which is 'common to us all . . . what I would call the "jealousies" of the different faiths. I mean those points in every religion concerning which the believers are inwardly compelled to claim a universal significance and finality'. And he goes on to plead with those who are looking for a quick reconciliation between different faiths: 'leave us at least our capacity for categorical assertion, for that is what we have in common.'[8] He sees, that is to say, a claim to universality and finality as a characteristic of all, or at least most religions, and something therefore that should be maintained by both sides in any dialogue, without expectation of any diminution of its categorical character.

The objection needs to be taken seriously, for it is indeed the dialogue of the committed that really matters. But can it be allowed to stand without any diminution of *its* categorical character? For as it stands, it would seem to rule out not only the 'quick reconciliation' against which John Taylor is inveighing, but any long-term reconciliation as well. And it is hard to see how John Taylor could rest content with such a conclusion, for in the same article he himself affirms the belief 'that the ultimate reality upon which the faith of all believers is focused in every religion is the same, though our interpretations of his essential nature are still at variance'.[9] The conflicting 'categorical assertions' to which each attaches 'a universal significance and finality' are not about different realities but about the same reality. The Christian conviction that there is one God from whom all thoughts of truth proceed militates against the permanent acceptance of such a state of affairs. For that would be to add a further conflict to the conflict between the religions – namely a conflict between acquiescence in that conflict as a feature of God's world that we do not seek to change and the Christian's understanding of God as the sole and self-consistent source of all truth. Dialogue between religions which make conflicting categorical assertions is, as Taylor would be the first to agree, clearly called for. And while it is important that this should not lead to faith, in John Macquarrie's words, being 'levelled down to an indifference in which anything worthy to be called a faith-commitment has been silently suppressed',[10] it is also important that the goal of seeking to eliminate the element of conflict from the conflicting categorical claims be not silently suppressed either. And that surely implies that the dialogue has to be one which involves a process of mutual learning and readiness for self-correction. But the question remains: is such a process conceivable in view of the extent of conflicting categorical assertions?

To answer that question, we need to reflect on the religious use of language, without which no categorical assertion can be made. Religious language is a theme which receives more attention in the discussion of the philosophy of religion than in the consideration of doctrine or in the give and take of ecumenical encounter. Yet it is absolutely crucial to both those latter spheres. All our language about God is imagistic or symbolic. No form of language can provide us with correct descriptions of God. What we do in speaking about God is to take certain basic symbols and build them up by a process of symbolization so that they can point in particular ways to the transcendent reality of God. Surface-level conflicts – God is shepherd; God is rock – may turn out to be no conflict at all, when the way the language functions is properly understood. Conversely, the same symbol may have a variety of implications. Water can speak of the destructive power of the overwhelming flood or of the life-giving property of the refreshing draught – the waters of the Exodus in which the Egyptians were drowned or the springs of water in the desert whereby the lives of the Israelites were preserved. And, as that example shows, symbols can draw their strength either from certain universal characteristics appertaining to them (the destructive and sustaining properties of water) or from some particular historical occurrence in which those properties have been at work. In either case their strength derives from some shared experience.[11]

But the historical dimension in religious language is not just a matter of that language having its roots in some particular shared historical experience in the past. It is a matter of the way in which the language (however it may have first arisen) goes on being used at crucial moments in the continuing history of the community. The primary locus in which religious language functions, that is to say, is not the individual but an ongoing historical community.

It needs to be emphasized that this insistence on the symbolic character of religious language and the process of human construction by which it is developed is independent of any judgment we may make about divine revelation being communicated through it. But whatever our precise understanding of revelation may be, it seems simply absurd to claim that the language or concepts in which it is expressed are to be understood as themselves given in some purely transcendent way. They are the same culturally conditioned language and concepts which are in use over the whole range of human experience, and whose gradual development and modification can be traced over the centuries. They may be the medium of revelation, but they cannot be the direct and immediate embodiment of it.

So when John Taylor speaks about 'those points in every religion concerning which believers are inwardly compelled to claim a universal significance and finality', we need to ask whether he has phrased the matter quite correctly. It is only in so far as the 'points' are 'pointers' that we are justified in describing their significance in such absolute terms. They cannot have universality or finality in themselves; they can have it only in so far as they serve as pointers to the transcendent. It is God who is absolute, not the assertions that we make about him. That distinction is vital for the spiritual health of all religions, each of which needs to be defended against the dangerous tendency to idolatry.

The strongest emphasis on the indirectness and limitation of all human language about God within Christian history is to be seen in the apophatic tradition, with its insistence that such language properly tells us, not what God is, but what he is not: he is *in*finite, *in*generate, *im*mortal, *in*corporeal, *in*visible. Our firmest affirmations constitute a denial that God shares our human limitations. What it means to transcend those limitations is something we can only hint at indirectly. The continuation of that emphasis is vital to inter-religious dialogue. It is no coincidence that Nicholas of Cusa, whom I have already cited as perhaps the outstanding example of a sympathetic appraisal of other religions in the course of earlier Christian history, belonged to that tradition. His most famous work is entitled '*De Docta Ignorantia*' – on learned ignorance. In it he insists continually on the limitations of human language.

> It is necessary for him who wants to attain understanding to raise the intellect above the meaning of words, rather than to insist on the properties of words, which cannot be properly adapted to such great intellectual mysteries.[12]

And that, although it might sound like it at first hearing, is no flight from reason. E.F. Jacob describes Nicholas' aim as being to restore – or attempt to restore – the balance of reason and emotion by weighting once more the scale of reason, while at the same time demonstrating the limitations of the rational method.[13]

That aim finds vivid expression in Nicholas' own image of the intellect as being to truth as an inscribed polygon is to the inscribing circle.[14] No language about God, however hallowed, can claim the kind of completeness that would place it above any need of correction or supplementation from the language of others. Its role always and necessarily remains that of an indirect pointer to something that it cannot adequately or accurately express.

Moreover, we have also seen that the way these pointers point is not punctiliar. That is to say, their meaning is not given, nor do they function as pointers to truth, just on the basis of the particular occasion on which they are being used. Images build up associations over time in the context of specific religious communities. In speaking earlier about the role of experience in relation to religious knowledge, I emphasized how such experience comes to be codified in traditional patterns of language, and how such cumulative linguistic traditions contribute to subsequent experience and circumscribe the forms that it is likely to take. Every religious community, that is to say, develops a language peculiar to itself, whose full meaning will not be immediately apparent to those who approach it from outside. It has to be learnt. Most people will have had some lesser form of that experience: if, for example, one goes to stay with a close-knit family, it may well become evident that the language they use between themselves, though understandable enough at one level, carries a further level of meaning that eludes one. This emphasis on the way in which language is so intimately tied up with its use in a particular society has been the subject of a good deal of study – under the title of socio-linguistics. Recognition of the phenomenon has helped to illuminate and further the process of ecumenical understanding. It is no coincidence that its most notable application to Christian doctrine, George Lindbeck's book, *The Nature of Doctrine*,[15] was in large measure the outcome of sustained ecumenical encounter between Lutherans and Catholics, and was conceived as a creative contribution to further catholic-protestant rapprochement. Recognition of this characteristic of religious language is equally important to any assessment of the practical possibility of inter-religious dialogue.

But there are dangers to be guarded against in this approach, as well as valuable insights to be gained. Sometimes it has been used to suggest that different religious communities are impervious to one another. Under the influence of an extreme form of neo-Wittgensteinian philosophy, the implication has been drawn that the languages built up over the years by different communities make communication between them an impossibility. But while different religious communities, as I have been arguing, certainly do develop their own language in particular ways, they are not totally opaque to those who belong to another community. Catholic-protestant dialogue and rapprochement have not proved impossible, even though they have not been entirely straightforward either. The complexity of the process derives in large measure from the rich associations that the characteristic language and the particular practices of each tradition have built up over the centuries. The same principle applies in the case of inter-religious dialogue. There, of course, the cumulative linguistic traditions of the different religions are far more divergent in character. The complexities of the process

37

will be vastly greater than in the case of ecumenical encounter. But by the same token a recognition of the socio-linguistic grounding of their radical divergence provides a basis for hope. The conflicting character of the categorical assertions each now makes from within its own relatively isolated existence need not, it suggests, imply that the whole process is doomed from the outset. There is a road that enables us to move beyond the apparent confrontation of absolute opposites. And in taking that road, we will not find ourselves stranded in a cul-de-sac of inescapable mutual incomprehension.

But there is another way in which the socio-linguistic approach can be exaggerated with misleading effect. Important as its insights are, they do not automatically do away with the referential element in religious discourse, as is sometimes supposed. Just because the form of a particular community's language about God is very largely a construct, whose shape has been determined by the historical conditions and experience of that community, it does not follow that God has no reality other than as a way of speaking about the community's experience. It only means that the process of understanding *how* that language applies to the reality of God will be even more indirect and more elusive than it would anyway have been because of the symbolic nature of the language used. It would admittedly be tempting to play down the referential element altogether in inter-religious dialogue. For the conflicts there are of a different order from those encountered in ecumenical dialogue. We are faced, indeed, not only with the conflict between personal and impersonal ideas of God (something very close to that can after all be found within Christian thought itself), but even with the repudiation of the concept of God altogether. But we are not free to eliminate the referential element simply in order to facilitate the process of dialogue. The dialogue is not a matter of negotiating a better relation between two ways of speaking and living religiously, which are at our disposal to do whatever we like with; it is a shared search for truth. If the referential element in religious language is to be diminished or abandoned, it must be on other grounds than the potential usefulness of doing so to the cause of inter-religious dialogue. For my part I do not find those other grounds convincing.

But with such diverse understandings of God to be found in different religions (and even, indeed, the repudiation of the concept of God altogether), is the maintenance of a referential element in religious language consistent with the kind of dialogue I am envisaging? Since there are such radical differences between their accounts of the transcendent, will we not be bound to treat the majority of them as false and misleading human constructions, whose accounts lack the requisite referential element? If reference could only be secured by an accurate description of the object to which reference is intended, then we might find ourselves forced to adopt such a conclusion. But that mode of securing reference is not the only possible one, and is particularly inappropriate in the religious context. Many philosophers prefer a causal theory of reference, in which reference is secured not by a correct definition of the object in question but by the causal-historical relations which link the speaker with the intended referent. Different groups of hunters may all sight the same, previously unknown species of animal. They may all give it different names and offer widely divergent descriptions, each perhaps containing substantial inaccuracies. The differences may arise partly from the different nature of the sightings and partly from long-established differences in methods of tracking and hunting. Yet all their divergently inaccurate descriptions clearly have a referent and serve as effective means of reference. In an interesting article in *Faith and Philosophy*, Richard Miller has argued that this way of understanding how our language refers makes it easier to understand how the divergent, even conflicting, affirmations of the different religions may yet refer to the same, one God. 'God of the Hebrews, God of the Arabs, God of the Hindus ... could all be different names for the same being *even if there is no significant overlap in belief about His nature*'.[16] The differences of description are real and important, but they do not determine reference. That is determined by the causal-historical relations which have led the various traditions to speak of God – or even of some impersonal reality such as 'Tao' or Nirvana. And in that respect they may prove to have a good deal more in common. We must not claim too much for this illustration. It does not and is not intended to minimize the deep differences between such varied conceptions of that which is religiously ultimate. It is intended simply to suggest that we are not forced to choose between either on the one hand denying the referential character of religious language altogether or on the other acquiescing in the ineradicable incompatibility of differing religious faiths. Despite the differences in their descriptions (within which there may well be much error), they may all genuinely refer to one transcendent reality, even though they name and describe that reality in such mutually inconsistent ways.

The formidable nature of the conflicting categorical assertions of the differing religions is certainly not to be underestimated. But they need not, I am arguing, be seen as an insuperable barrier to the kind of dialogue I am advocating. It is a common experience in individual religious development, that what has been apprehended as an absolute and inalienable part of a person's Christian belief may in the course of time come into conflict with other beliefs he or she holds about the world. Such occasions may seem at first to be occasions for despair, but they can prove to be opportunities for personal growth.[17] The same has been true of the ecumenical movement. Can it be true also in the case of inter-religious dialogue?

An affirmative answer to that question depends on a proper recognition of the dynamic, historical character of all religions. If religions are understood as fixed systems of belief, then the conflicting nature of their categorical assertions will inevitably appear as an unsurmountable bar to their rapprochement. Reflection on the nature of religious language of the kind that I have been pursuing may perhaps mitigate the directness of that conflict in some respects. But by itself it will hardly serve to resolve the difficulty. Even when due allowance has been made for that factor, the conflicting character of the affirmations of the different religions remains the dominant impression. And so, it is likely to be argued, in the interest of truth opposition must remain the dominant characteristic of their relation to one another. It is thus a very proper concern for truth which lies at the heart of much resistance to the idea of an open inter-religious dialogue of the kind that I am proposing. It is widely assumed that if such dialogue is to make any progress it will have to involve either an abdication of any claim to truth on the part of one of the religions involved, or else abandonment of any claim to cognitive content on the part of religious affirmations generally.

I have already argued that that is not a necessary corollary of recognizing the socio-linguistic character of religious language and religious beliefs, and that the radical differences in the various religions' accounts of the transcendent do not disprove the possibility that all may have one and the same referent. But I want now to put the point more positively. The strong form of the objection that an open approach to inter-religious dialogue sets a low premium on truth in religion arises directly out of a falsely static view of the nature of religion. This is exemplified by the climax of an article by Roger Trigg, entitled 'Religion and the Threat of Relativism'. He ends the article with these words:

> The future of religion is deservedly in jeopardy when no clear answers can in principle be given to such questions as . . . 'Is Christianity true?' A refusal by any religion to claim truth can be as devastating as an admission of its falsity.[18]

If Christianity is understood as essentially a set of assertions about what is the case, then the demand for a clear answer to the question 'Is Christianity true?' is appropriate. But if Christianity is understood as an interpretation of the world with some grasp of truth, but above all with a commitment to the continued search for truth, the appropriateness of putting the demand in that way is not so obvious. Indeed I want to claim that the implication of a serious concern for truth in religion as it bears on the question of inter-religious dialogue is the opposite of what it is normally assumed to be. In the light of how our present limited apprehension of truth has been built up, it is only if we are prepared to enter into such dialogue – and so take account of as full a range of human religious experience as possible – that we will be in a position to lay claim to a serious concern for truth. Certainly we must not deny what we believe to be true in our own religion for the sake of easier relations with others; but the greater danger is that we will fail to acknowledge the modifications and qualifications that are needed in the formulation of the faith by which we ourselves live. In other words what is called for is a strongly revisionist understanding of religious belief, according to which truth is the goal rather than the present possession of every religion.

Whether such a process of revision will in fact lead to a deeper grasp of religious truth in which the affirmations of the different religions (appropriately revised in substance and in the mode of their interpretation) will prove to be complementary and compatible cannot be known in advance. Nor can the particular form of mutual learning and self-correction that such a process may involve. That belongs to the theology *of* dialogue rather than the theology *for* dialogue, with which I am concerned here. As yet, it lies well outside the sphere of anyone's experience, let alone mine. What I am wanting to claim at this stage is that a serious concern for Christian truth requires us to embark on such a course, like Abraham to go out in faith, not knowing where it is that we may be led.

But there is a preliminary question, which does belong to this first stage of a theology for dialogue. I have argued that it is impossible for Christians to rule out in advance the truth of all other religions and to claim to know, on the basis of what has already been given to them in their own faith, that truth belongs exlusively to them. We may have been dragged reluctantly, even perhaps kicking and screaming, to this recognition by the practical need for better relations between the religions, which is so evident a feature of our time. But my claim has been that having been forced to face the issue afresh, it is possible to make out a strong case that the logic of Christian faith itself requires us to embark on a genuinely open dialogue. We do not and should not modify the form of our own faith to simplify the difficult process on which we are being called to embark. As Jürgen Moltmann has put it, 'as a Muslim I believe I would have little interest in a Christianity that makes vital concessions before entering into conversation with me'.[19] But if, as I have argued, there has always been a revisionary character to Christianity down the ages, a Christianity which denied the propriety of any future change to its existing beliefs would be an equally unsatisfactory dialogue partner. And there is one task which, in the light of all that has been said so far, is incumbent on the Christian who is convinced of the propriety of inter-religious dialogue, even before he starts on the dialogue itself. How, in the context of a more open attitude to the truths inherent in other religions, ought we to view the existing resources of Christian theology? That theology has always been open to change. Are there aspects of it that, at least as commonly understood, stand in conflict with such readiness for dialogue? And, if there are, do they need to be modified, not by way of concession in the interest of a smoother dialogue but by way of necessity in the interest of consistency and truth? That is the question I propose to tackle in the next chapter, and it will lead us to deal more directly than I have done so far with the crucial question of how we may best understand the person of Christ himself in such a context.

3

A Test Case: The Theology of Karl Rahner

The task I set myself at the end of the previous chapter was to consider how far Christian theology, as it is now affirmed and understood, is compatible with the proposal I have been making for radically open dialogue with other religions. The task is a somewhat speculative one, because we cannot know in advance what course such dialogue may take and cannot therefore know precisely what its implications for Christian theology may turn out to be. But we can spell out in general terms the implications of embarking on such a dialogue at all, and at that general level the question of the compatibility of those implications with existing Christian self-understanding is a proper subject for review. Just because of the inescapably speculative character of the discussion, it is important that it should not simply take the form of one individual's private fantasy, carefully tailored to produce the desired result. It needs to be anchored to the work of Christian theology already known and respected in the public domain. Christian theology is, of course, incurably diverse – not least on the particular issue at stake here. I have chosen as my starting-point for this next stage of our enquiry the work of Karl Rahner. In doing do, I am of course choosing somebody who has been much concerned with Christianity's relation to the non-Christian religions.

But that has not been the dominating or controlling motif in his theological work, as it has been with some other twentieth-century writers whom I might have chosen for the purpose. It has been a part, albeit an important part, of a much wider concern. Rahner's overall aim has been to provide a reasoned and coherent theology that is genuinely responsive to the insights of our time while also standing squarely within the Catholic tradition. Those three features of all Rahner's work – a well-worked out and coherent intellectual structure, a sensitivity to the intellectual challenges of the modern world and a deeply religious commitment to church tradition – make it particularly appropriate to our present purpose.

Karl Rahner was a prolific and highly technical writer. But underlying the very precise, and often very difficult, detail was a consistency of vision that makes it possible, as I shall be doing here, to assess the cumulative thrust of his work without having to concern oneself too much with all the niceties of his precise presentation of his position. The question I shall be asking is how far his overall theological vision is hospitable to the open dialogue that I am proposing. In so far as it is, we will have found what we are looking for – namely, a way in which Christian theology may be seen to support the development of open dialogue with other religious traditions, and also a theological framework into which it may prove possible to accommodate particular new insights arising out of that dialogue. In so far as it is not, we will have to ask whether it lends itself to appropriate modification or development, without either destroying its overall coherence or removing it altogether from its place within Christian tradition. Whichever assessment our discussion should lead to, there remains a good prospect that it may provide a useful basis for the attempt to spell out more fully my own understanding in the final chapter.

A contemporary Christian theology cannot simply assume the reality of God. That is true of any theology in the post-Christian West; it is particularly true of a theology which seeks to be open to other religious traditions, where the reality of God may be very differently understood, if it is acknowledged at all. Of course in the substantive working out of that theology, one will go on to speak freely of God. In no system of belief does one need to justify its key terms every time they are used, even though their precise significance or the reality of that to which they refer may be far from self-evident to every one. But what is vital is that the way the term God is used within a theology should be consistent with the way in which an underlying faith in God is understood to be grounded.

Rahner is well aware of that requirement. For him the grounding of faith in God is to be found in the realm of anthropology, in reflection on what is involved in the fundamental fact of our existence as human selves. Since our existence is essentially historical in character – that is to say, none of us just exists in a general or universal way, but each of us exists as particular people in particular historical circumstances – the starting-point of such reflection can only be the particular historical circumstances that have come our way. But the goal of our reflection has to be to go beyond those particular, contingent experiences themselves and identify the underlying realities or structures that make *any* distinctively human experience possible. These Rahner designates 'existentials'. They are to be firmly distinguished from the particular experiences themselves, even though it is only possible for us to get at them through the medium of those particular experiences. How can such a process of reflection be carried out?

Suppose we put to ourselves the question: what constitutes us the particular persons that we are? There are a variety of factors on which we can call to provide information towards the answering of that question. We can draw on knowledge of our genetic inheritance, and of the environment in which we have been brought up and now live. But any answers of this kind we may come up with only serve to pose more questions. The more we recognize the significance of our origins, genetic and environmental, the more puzzling becomes our apparent freedom and our sense of responsibility for what we make or fail to make of that inheritance. To deny that we have any such freedom or responsibility is not only to go against a fundamental aspect of our experience; even more importantly it is to deny what is most distinctively human about us. We cannot get away from the question: how are we able to contribute to shaping what is apparently given to us in our origins? How is it that we can 'make something of ourselves'? Who is the 'we' who is both subject and object of this making something of ourselves? Reflection on these questions is likely to lead to the conclusion that, inescapable as they are, they are incapable of being answered, because any answer arising from within the system of acquiring knowledge with which we have to work is bound to generate yet further questions. And so we are forced on into an awareness of the 'infinite question which encompasses us', a question that can be described either as unanswerable or as its own answer. This inescapable road of 'self-transcendence' shows us that human life has an ineluctable 'orientation towards mystery'. And God is the name for that 'absolute mystery' towards which this distinctively human style of reflection inevitably points.

Rahner's appeal is not just to occasions of profound solitary introspection. It is to something that underlies the whole range of human, and therefore social, life. It includes, for example, appeal to what is implicit in such experiences as the unconditional character of love given or love received, and the sense of responsibility for one's actions in what is apprehended as an absolute moral imperative. At the heart of all these distinctively human experiences are indicators, Rahner believes, of an all-embracing and inconceivable mystery. I have described the process of reflection which can give rise to awareness of that mystery in highly intellectual terms (even if not quite so sophisticated intellectual terms as Rahner himself employs), but Rahner insists that the experience itself is not dependent for its reality on such intellectual formulation. He argues that it should be recognized as present, as a form of 'unthematic awareness', even in the most rudimentary forms of genuinely human experience. Primitive burial customs, for example, he suggests, are evidence of the presence of this orientation towards mystery long before it was ever spelt out in any reasoned form.[1]

All that I have been describing so far is intended by Rahner as an analysis of what is implied by human existence as such. It is offered as a form of philosophical reflection with no explicit Christian assumptions involved. 'Orientation towards mystery' is implicit in all genuinely human forms of experience. But as a theologian Rahner wants to say more. Corresponding to this universal human 'orientation towards mystery' is an equally universal offer of divine self-communication. That Rahner designates a 'supernatural existential'. It is an 'existential' because what is being referred to are not particular occasions of God's approach to human beings in the historical phenomenon of Christianity, or of any other religion; it is something

49

universal, a characteristic ingredient of all human existence. But it is a '*supernatural* existential', because it is a
purely gratuitous self-offering of God to human beings,
additional to and going beyond that which constitutes
human nature as such. God's presence as question, which
is knowable by philosophical reflection on human existence as such, is, we might say, supplemented by God's
presence as answer, which is knowable only by reflection
on the history of revelation, but which is nonetheless
something true of all existence, whether recognized and
responded to or not.

Where then are we to locate this 'history of revelation',
through which the offer of divine self-communication is
to be known? Traditionally Christians have identified it
with the biblical story of God's dealings with his chosen
people from the time of the call of Abraham onwards. But
since for Rahner the offer of divine self-communication is
universal, and the address whereby God makes possible a
relation between himself and human persons is an inalienable element in all human existence, its history cannot be
so restricted in scope. Potentially at least it is coexistent
with the history of the world. In practice it is the history
of human responses, however imperfect, to that offer; it
is the history of the ways, however inadequate, in which
it has been recognized and expressed in human language
and custom. And that history is not just the history of
individual occasions of divine self-communication and
human response. All human experience, as we have seen
in the earlier chapters, arises within and is significantly
influenced by a continuing tradition in which it stands.
In this case the divine self-communication and human
responses to it have been interpreted and found expression
in a variety of forms in different religious communities.
So what Christians have been accustomed to speak of as

'the history of revelation' or 'salvation history', namely the historical development recorded in Old and New Testaments that found its climax in Jesus, is not salvation history as such; it is one development of it – not the only one, but the one that in the eyes of Christians has led to the full instantiation of divine offer and human response in the person of Jesus.

What this framework enables us to recognize is that different religious traditions may represent different articulations of the underlying, universal offer of divine self-communication. And many of the differences between them may be due to the ways in which differing forms of historical experience have led to the use and development of different images or symbols as fundamental pointers to the transcendent reality of God. That does not, of course, imply that all such developments are equally adequate, or that there do not or could not exist genuine conflicts between them. It does, however, imply that there is an immensely complex task of discrimination required to distinguish between the various differences that are to be found between differing religions. In some cases those differences may involve intractably incompatible understandings of our world and of that transcendent reality in which it is grounded, where one (or more probably both) are in need of substantial correction. In other cases, however, the differences may turn out to be primarily the outcome of a use of different images, related to different historical and cultural experiences, and not prove in the long run to constitute the radical conflict they seemed at first to present.

On this basis Rahner is able to assert 'that non-Christian religions . . . can be realities *within* a *positive* history of salvation and revelation'. The existence of revelation and real faith outside the Christian sphere is not for him something that happens occasionally apart from, or even in spite of, other religions. It occurs '*concretely* and *on the whole* only by the mediation of those categorial, institutional and verbal realities which we know as non-Christian religions'.[2] Indeed if any acknowledgment is to be made of divine self-communication and genuine human response in the case of individual members of other religions, that religion has to be seen as a positive contribution to that encounter of faith. Not to do so would be to understand the encounter in non-social and unhistorical terms, and that would be to fly in the face of the social and historical nature of all human existence.[3]

But Rahner is equally clear about the priority and superiority of the Christian tradition. The full text of the passage about non-Christian religions being realities within a positive history of salvation and revelation from which I have just quoted, qualifies the reference to non-Christian religions with the words; 'even though incomplete, rudimentary and partially debased'.

Rahner's confident assertion of the superiority of Christian revelation is based on his understanding of the person of Jesus. For him, Jesus embodies the perfect coming together of divine self-offering and human response, which in its imperfection constitutes the underlying form of the whole history of human existence understood religiously. Indeed that way of putting it, that Jesus embodies the perfect coming together of divine self-offering and human response, though true as far as it goes, understates the claim that Rahner makes about Jesus. Jesus is not just one instantiation of the goal of God's purpose in the creation of the world; nor just the first; not even the only full embodiment of it so far. The coming together of the divine and the human in Jesus is final and unrepeatable. It is 'something which must happen once, and once only, at the point where the world begins to enter into its final phase'.[4] It is 'the "final cause" of God's universal self-communication to the world'.[5]

Such a strong conviction about the unique and final place of Jesus in the history of God's dealings with the world does not combine easily with Rahner's other strong conviction that there is a real history of divine salvation at work in other religious traditions. If Christ is the indispensable medium of divine salvation, how can that salvation be attainable within other religious traditions that are either ignorant of him or that reject the claims that are made about him? It was struggle with that dilemma that gave rise to Rahner's most idiosyncratic and most debated contribution to the whole area of discussion with which we are concerned. Since Christ is for him the irreplacable norm of all God's dealings with the world, Christ must be the truth that lies behind those other developments of the history of salvation, which constitute the other great religious traditions of the world. And so Rahner spoke of those whom he saw as genuinely responding to God's self-communication in the context of another religion as 'anonymous Christians'. Christ is seen as the God-given reality, of which every other genuine (but by definition imperfect) occasion of a meeting of the human and the divine is a partial copy. From a Christian confessional standpoint, of course, one could not find a higher evaluation of another religious tradition. But it is hardly surprising if it is not readily heard that way by the other partner in any potential dialogue, who by definition does not share that confessional standpoint.

I do not propose to add directly to the already extensive discussion of that particular phrase. My allusion to it was introduced as an illustration of the more fundamental tension in Rahner's thought between his insistence on the absolute finality and indispensability of Christ and his positive evaluation of other religious traditions as conveying divine salvation. And that, in its turn, is a particular form of a still more general tension, which any sensitive theologian is bound to experience, between what Schubert Ogden calls the criteria of 'appropriateness' and 'credibility', between faithfulness to the heart of Christian tradition and responsiveness to the intellectual and moral challenges of the present. And that is a tension that suffuses all Rahner's writings. In the critical discussion of his handling of that tension, it will be important not simply to cut the Gordian knot and abandon concern for one of the two poles. But the exploration of the possibility of some revision of Rahner's position seems worth undertaking. We have already seen the need for a revisionary approach to theology in general as a form of faithfulness to the tradition, and Rahner's work is itself a notable example of such an approach. A revisionary theologian can hardly object to attempts to provide further revision of his own proposals. I hope to be able to point to a number of respects in which Rahner's revisionary approach can be taken a stage further in a way that will make it more coherent, as well as more open to other religions, without taking it right outside the stream of Christian tradition.

'If we wish to be Christians, we must profess belief in the universal and serious salvific purpose of God towards all men.' I quoted those words of Rahner at a much earlier stage of the discussion as an example of a statement that is both old and new.[6] It sums up the underlying Christian conviction that God is love, and wills all men to be saved and to come to a knowledge of the truth. But it does so in the context of a new consciousness both of the size and of the interconnectedness of our world. It is a basic religious conviction which underlies all Rahner's work, and finds specific expression in his concept of the 'supernatural existential'. But the distinction that Rahner makes, which is encapsulated in that designation, between God's creative relationship to human life and this additional, special relationship, which is none the less also universal, is an awkward one. John Robertson summarizes Rahner's view like this:

> It is in principle possible that all [man] could know would be God's silence. *In fact*, God has elected to love man, and hence man is in a state of grace as well as nature.[7]

And Rahner himself admits that

> Our actual nature is *never* 'pure' nature . . . It is continually being determined . . . by the supernatural grace of salvation offered to it.[8]

It is not surprising, therefore, that a number of his critics have asked whether such a distinction, involving the wholly theoretical construct of a 'pure' human nature, is either necessary or possible.[9] It is not difficult to see the point that Rahner wants to make. God's relation to the world is never anything less than a 'universal and serious salvific pupose'; it is the same Holy Spirit or supernatural grace, which is the source and substance of the Christian's salvation in the church, that 'exists as such always and everywhere and therefore also outside institutional Christianity';[10] it is not some lower order of divine self-communication that is on offer in that wider context. Nor is it difficult to see why Rahner expresses himself in this convoluted manner. He is seeking to be faithful to the particular Catholic tradition in which he stands with its contrasting categories of nature and supernature. But that distinction is designed to differentiate at precisely the point where Rahner wants to unite. They are, therefore, categories in terms of which his point *can* only be made in an unconvincingly convoluted manner. God's creative activity is an expression of his love, and his offer of divine self-communication is the meaning and purpose of the creation, not some kind of secondary supplementation to it, which just happens 'in fact' to be the case. Rahner's point can be made more tellingly by doing away with the distinction, and speaking more straightforwardly of the universality of the address of the divine love as at the heart of all human existence, and a fundamental aspect of it.

A modification of that kind to Rahner's scheme of thought does not make any great difference to the issue that is central to our concern. But it is instructive as indicating the kind of change that may be appropriate – a greater readiness to modify traditional categories of expression and belief in order to do better justice to the insights that he himself sees as arising out of our more recent experience. A second, and for our purpose, more significant inconsistency, which once again has been pointed out by a number of his critics, relates to his understanding of the person of Christ.

History is the history of God's gracious offer of self-communication to men and women. And it is emphatically a matter of *offer*; men and women are free to ignore it or to reject it, as well as to accept it. This respect for human freedom characterizes all God's dealings with the world. History and nature fall within the sphere of God's gracious self-offering, since that is universal in its scope. So grace does not override them in order to make room for divine self-communication. Even miracles, for example, are not to be understood preternaturally (as divine alteration of the processes of nature), but theologically (as events in which the divine self-communication becomes particularly clear and effective). God's salvific acts are never simply done *to* men and women, without at the same time being the acts *of* those human persons. And the goal of this whole process, the purpose of all history, and more specifically of the history of revelation understood as the history of human awareness and partial response to the divine offer, is its completion in the perfect coming together of divine offer and human response. And this, it is claimed, has indeed happened in the person of Christ. In the context of this general understanding of God's way of acting in the world Rahner can do more justice to the traditional orthodox affirmation of the humanity of Christ than most theologians of a similarly traditional temper succeed in doing. Christ's humanity is not suppressed or diminished in any way by his divinity. Since that orientation towards the mystery of God, which is the essence of all human potential and the guarantee of our fundamental freedom, is completely fulfilled in Christ, he is in fact the most free of all human beings. At the same time Rahner can present Jesus as the perfect coming together of the divine and the human; in other words, as one who corresponds to the account given by the traditional incarnational doctrine of the hypostatic union.

But while that picture can certainly claim real continuity with important aspects of christological tradition, there are other important aspects which it does not incorporate. For Christ is also affirmed in the tradition to be unique, final and indispensable as the medium of salvation. And, as we have seen, Rahner emphatically endorses that element of the tradition as well. But as critics have pointed out, it is not easy to see how he is in a position to do so. As Gerken puts it:

It would be more consistent if one drew the conclusion from Rahner's view that every historical event, with respect to its ability to bring the graciously elevated transcendentality of man to self-realization, is of equal value and that, therefore, even the Christ event and the form of Christ are replaceable.[11]

And Bruce Marshall argues similarly that Rahner's more general theological method

is radically inconsistent with his own most basic commitments about the place of Jesus Christ as a particular person in the Christian belief in redemption and a redeemer.[12]

I do not think there is any escape from these accusations of inconsistency. Some modification of Rahner's position seems unavoidable if it is to maintain its avowed aim of providing a reasoned and intellectually coherent account of Christian belief. Marshall's choice is to opt for Rahner's christological conviction and reject his theological method. But that is in effect to abandon Rahner as a theological guide altogether, and to adopt in its place, as Marshall does, something more akin to the theological approach of Karl Barth.

If one prefers to take the other option and stay with Rahner's more general theological method, while abandoning the christological conviction that he maintains, can one give supporting reasons for contemplating a modification of Rahner's scheme at that particular point? The christological conviction that he upholds is the traditional doctrine of incarnation or hypostatic union – including, as we have seen, the insistence that Christ so conceived is unique and final; and the particular characteristic of our modern outlook with which Rahner wants to demonstrate its harmony is an evolutionary understanding of the world. The title of one of his articles from which I have already quoted is 'Christology within an Evolutionary View of the World'.[13] He is conscious that, on the face of it, christology and an evolutionary view of the world represent 'two completely unrelated lines of thought', but he sets out to demonstrate their 'inner affinity' and 'the possibility of their being mutually related'.[14] I have already accepted that in his presentation of Christ as the climax of a gradual process of human self-transcendence by way of response to divine self-communication, he goes some way towards achieving that aim. But at the same time I have argued that his attempt to present the incarnation as necessarily unique, final and unrepeatable in its bringing this meeting of the divine and the human to perfection at a particular point in that evolutionary development seems unconvincing. A broadly evolutionary understanding certainly allows room for the emergence of the genuinely new, a *metabasis eis allo genos* of the kind Rahner understands the incarnation to be. But it does not seem able to allow for that new emergent to be final and unrepeatable, which is also for Rahner a part of the understanding of the incarnation. Is continued insistence on that aspect of the understanding of incarnation an essential element in Christian faithfulness?

Certainly it has been a major constituent in Christian tradition from early times. But even so it did not spring ready-made from the head of Zeus, or from the mouth of Yahweh. It is an interpretation of the significance of Jesus by very early followers of his, who, like all of us, devised their interpretation from within and in terms of the particular, contingent tradition in which they stood. Now one particularly striking difference between the general outlook of their age and ours is a difference in our respective views of history. The role of an apocalyptic expectation of an imminent end to world history in the formation of Jesus' own teaching and of the New Testament may have been overplayed, though for my part I do not see how it can be eliminated altogether in either case. Certainly Rahner speaks of Jesus' expressing himself 'by means of what we usually call apocalyptic, an imminent expectation and an eschatology of the present',[15] and of 'the vision of early Christianity [being] very limited with regard to both the past and future temporal extent of the history it had to interpret ... due to the very limited spatio-temporal horizon of its own historical existence'.[16] This foreshortened sense of history, together with the hope for some decisive action of God whereby his purpose for his people and for the world would shortly be brought to completion, is surely of the utmost significance for the way in which the transformative significance of Jesus was understood. In that conceptual context, to see Jesus as the final and irreplaceable medium of salvation is natural enough. But once we allow the general principle of a revisionary approach to Christian doctrine which takes account of well-established changes in our basic understanding of the world and of its history, the concept of Christ's finality and irreplaceability is surely a candidate for such rethinking. John Macquarrie puts the point clearly:

When Christianity was born in the first century, people supposed our earth to be at the centre of things, so that terrestrial history was cosmic history. Moreover this had been a short history, or at least short enough for people to know what had happened from 'the beginning' down to their own day, and it was all going to end soon. Thus it was natural enough to suppose that there might be one exclusive or at any rate immeasurably superior revelation in the course of this short history.[17]

Yet Rahner's faithfulness to church tradition leads him to hold on to a christological conviction of Christ's uniqueness, finality and unrepeatability without any modification arising from considerations of that kind. It is little wonder that for all its sophistication and its valuable insights, his *tour de force* in trying to demonstrate its 'inner affinity' with an evolutionary view of the world, does not finally succeed.

It needs to be added that there is also a more general and more familiar problem which relates to the other aspect of Rahner's christology that I have discussed, where I acknowledged that there was not the same conflict with his general theological method or with his desire to present his theology as fully consistent with an evolutionary view of the world. What fits so well into Rahner's overall scheme is, as he himself, acknowledges 'the *idea* of the God-man' as the completion of the process of human self-transcendence. But in Rahner's view 'the salvation of man does not depend merely on the idea but also on the contingent, concrete facts of real history'; one cannot be a Christian (other, presumably, than an anonymous one) without 'the acknowledgment of Jesus and of no one else as the one, unique and real God-man'.[18] But how is one to base one's acknowledgment of Jesus as having lived out a perfect and complete union of divine offer and human response? Rahner is fully cognizant of the variety of exegetical conclusion about Jesus reached by different scholars, and how much less the evidence at our disposal is able to tell us about the inner dispositions of Jesus than used at one time to be supposed. Rahner speaks of the acknowledgment as a 'perception of faith'. But in that case is what we are enabled to acknowledge genuinely a matter of the 'concrete facts of real history'? And it is important for Rahner that it should be, because in his view it is precisely the actualization of God's absolute self-communication in history in the incarnation that is the 'definitive beginning and the absolute guarantee' that the goal of human self-transcendence will be brought to an ultimately successful conclusion.[19] It is, as I say, a familiar problem, but none the less real for that. If the way to both historical and religious knowledge necessarily has the kind of indirectness I have been arguing for, the form of that acknowledgment may need to be revised. It may still provide the basis for an appropriate expression of the absoluteness of a Christian's commitment to God as known through Jesus; but as a historical claim and as an irreformable expression of a Christian's commitment, it will surely need to be more open to possible revision.

The aim of this critical discussion of Rahner's christology has been to see what justification there might be for accepting his general theological approach, while seeking to modify his position on that particular score. For him it was certainly an important and integral feature of his theology, to which he was unflinchingly committed. But from my standpoint it constitutes a hindrance to any use of his theological framework as the basis for genuinely open inter-religious dialogue. Yet it would hardly be a satisfactory procedure to abandon it simply on that score. As I have been insisting throughout, that can never of itself be a sufficient ground for the modification of our Christian theology. My first aim, therefore, was to show that it led to an inconsistency within Rahner's own theology. I tried then to show, in addition to that, that if we accept the general principle that Christian doctrines which have taken their particular form on the basis of cultural assumptions that are no longer tenable may need to be revised in the light of a changed understanding of the world, then the form of Rahner's christological conviction is a strong candidate for such revision. There is thus a convergence of factors that can rightly encourage us to explore a theological vision which, while drawing much from Rahner's courageous and creative opening up of theology in the direction that is needed, may yet go beyond him at this point. In the final chapter I shall try to indicate what that theological vision might look like.

4

A Theology for Dialogue

In this final chapter I want to outline the general shape of a Christian theology appropriate to an acceptance of open inter-religious dialogue. For the most part it will be a drawing together of ideas that have been either explicit or implicit in the arguments developed so far.

More important than any specific aspects of the content of such a theology is the question of what status is to be ascribed to it. How should one describe the overall character of the theology we hope to construct? I want to suggest three adjectives that together serve to indicate its basic nature. It will need to be perspectival, parabolic and provisional. These features follow from the account given in Chapter 2 of the way theology appeals to the interpretation of experience within a tradition, the nature of religious language and the changing, historical character of human existence.

To say that a theology is perspectival is to acknowledge that it necessarily embodies a particular cultural approach to the world. To say that something has been 'revealed' does not imply that it escapes this necessity. Many believers assume that it does and some contemporary philosophers of religion support that assumption. But it is simply false to say, in the words of one such philosopher of religion, that there are things that can be known to be 'true without qualification' on the authority of a prophet who can be known to speak with the authority of God,[1] or, in the words of another, that 'once one believes God has really revealed something, one is bound to believe it on simple authority'.[2] Any revelation, real or otherwise, finds its expression in the context and the thought forms of some specific and contingent cultural tradition. All theology is in that sense perspectival. No manner of divine authorization can override that feature of the human situation.

To say that a theology is parabolic is to recall the special degree of indirectness with which any language refers to the divine or to the transcendent. Language, whose primary application is to the human sphere, is always being used in a stretched, or symbolic, or metaphorical way when it is applied to God. It can never, therefore, lay claim to being the one correct description of God in relation to the world. The concept of 'verbal inerrancy' in relation to theology is not merely false in fact but impossible in principle.

To say that a theology is provisional is to draw attention to the new knowledge about the world that is continually coming to light. That is not to commit oneself to some theory of inevitable and unerring progress. There is loss as well as gain, forgetting as well as new discovery. But it is impossible to deny that genuine new knowledge, however partial, about the physical, psychological and social worlds has come to light in recent centuries and will continue to do so. And it should be equally impossible to deny that in so far as such knowledge is genuine it must affect our theology, if that theology is about God's relation with this world and not with some fantasy world. So our theology is not only revisionary in that it seeks justifiably to revise the theologies of the past. It is also provisional in that it knows that it is itself always in need of revision. The truths formulated by theology are not eternal truths.

Those characterizations of theology have been expressed in terms of contemporary theological method. But they ought not to come as any surprise to those who express faith in the Holy Spirit. For they correspond to three distinctive characteristics of traditional understanding of the Spirit. The Spirit is given to the community and interprets that community's experience in relation to God; the Spirit gives access to a reality of God, which ordinary human words struggle falteringly to articulate both in prayer and in reflective speech; and the Spirit is the spirit of promise, the 'arrabon' or foretaste pointing forward to a future fulfilment as yet unrealized. The Spirit is witness to the perspectival, parabolic and provisional character of Christian life and thought.

More significantly those characterizations are derived from entirely general considerations of theological method and apply therefore to all forms of Christian theology. But they clearly have a special significance in relation to inter-religious dialogue. The perspectival character of theology means that there is *prima facie* room for a complementary theology from the different perspective of, for example, a Hindu understanding of the world. That is not to say that the differences between the two approaches are unreal or can be allowed simply to continue to co-exist without further ado. It is clear that there are genuine conflicts between them. But a recognition of the perspectival character of all theology enables us to see the existence of even radical difference as having the possibility of positive, and not simply negative, implications in relation to God's self-revelation to the world. It also enables those differences to be approached with a proper recognition of their complexity and at the same time with grounds for hope that their exploration may prove constructive for both religious traditions. The parabolic character of theology carries essentially the same implication over a narrower front. The indirectness of the way in which religious language refers does not eliminate the possibility of direct contradiction between different theologies or religious utterances. But it is a reminder that even direct verbal contradiction may be less absolute in reality than the purely verbal conflict suggests. Finally, and most importantly, the revisionary task, which is incumbent on every theology because of its provisional character, means that the discovery of difference and even of conflict need not be seen simply as a threat. It may prove to be the stimulus which opens up a valuable path of revision, for one or both of the conflicting religious traditions.

But my aim is not to speculate in advance about the particular forms of revision to which such a process might give rise for Christian theology at some future date. It is rather to consider what form of revision may be needed now to make such a process possible. And my discussion of Rahner's theology was intended as a first step towards such a consideration. In that discussion I expressed my general agreement with his emphasis on the universality of the divine offer of self-communication to the human creation. The major modification of his view that I proposed was to see that as even more integrally a part of God's creative work than is suggested by his separation of it out as a *supernatural* existential. I claimed indeed that my proposed modification seemed to do more justice to the main thrust even of his own thought, which I saw as awkwardly constrained at that point by the established categories of his particular tradition. Putting the point in its modified form is designed to express the claim that a part of what is meant by affirming that God is creator is to say that within and through the process of creation God makes himself accessible to a responsive relationship on the part of men and women. What is made possible is not just that men and women may be able to achieve a well-grounded conviction that there is a creator. The divine offer is an offer of self-communication. So it is not only an external knowledge about God that is possible; it is a relational knowledge of the kind that the biblical tradition equates with salvation or eternal life.

Clearly there is more to be said about the relation of that claim to traditional Christian doctrines of salvation. For the moment I want simply to make clear that it is insufficient to speak of a knowledge of God that is accessible universally, but a saving knowledge of God that is accessible only through the church and within the sphere of Christian faith. If God makes himself available to be known by way of a universal offer of divine self-communication, any knowledge of God arising from that potentiality is necessarily a saving knowledge. For divine self-communication implies more than an external knowledge of God's existence; it implies also whatever transformation of human life is required for human beings to enter into a true relationship with God. I do not think that that involves any very radical revision to the main tenor of contemporary Christian theology. A similar implication can be found, for example, in the affirmation of Christoph Schwöbel that 'it is the universality of God as the unconditional ground of all being and meaning which makes it necessary for Christian theology to acknowledge all religions, like the Christian religion, as human responses to the universal creative *and redeeming* agency of God'.[3] But it does involve a firm repudiation of some forms of past tradition, which are by no means dead yet. It is sometimes affirmed that, whatever may have been the

original divine intention for creation, any such general
divine address making possible a saving human response
has been withheld because of human sin and guilt. It has
even taken the form, as we saw earlier, of the denial that
God wills 'all men to be saved', and even the denial that he
enlightens 'everyone who comes into the world'.[4] Clearly
neither the position that I am advocating nor the one that
I am concerned to repudiate is open to empirical proof.
While accepting Rahner's claim that 'orientation towards
mystery' is a characteristic of all human existence as a
reasonable and persuasive one, I do not wish to under-
estimate the difficulty of making any universally applicable
affirmation about human existence. Certainly if Rahner's
claim is right, the universal divine address is heard in
widely differing ways and to greatly differing degrees. That
is the inevitable outcome of the great variety of cultural
and religious histories, since those histories provide the
medium through which the divine address comes to different communities and different individuals. But despite the
difficulties I have indicated, the kind of account that
Rahner offers has the advantage over most other accounts
of combining more effectively a broadly based reflection
on the forms of human experience with a view that is
consonant with the God of love apprehended in Jesus
Christ.

It may be objected that this general interpretation of
human existence is substantially influenced by my understanding of Christ as witness to the universal love of God.
That is true, but it is not an objection. It is a form of
Christian theology I am trying to articulate. It would only
be a valid objection if the understanding of Christ as
witness to the universal love of God stood in conflict with
the more general religious experience of mankind. We saw
an extreme form of that view earlier in the contrast drawn

by the neo-orthodox theologians between Christ as the revelation of God, and religion as a form of human construction constituting in reality a flight from God, and I gave my reasons for rejecting such a view.[5] It still finds expression of a less extreme kind in a writer like Lesslie Newbigin who argues that 'the wider religious, experience of mankind', symbolized by the rejection of Jesus as the enemy of God, is in 'radical discontinuity' with Christian faith and its apprehension of Jesus as Lord.[6] But even Newbigin has to admit that the discontinuity cannot be total. And were the discontinuity between Christian faith and all other forms of religious experience as radical as he suggests, it is hard to see how we could come to hold a justifiable faith in Jesus Christ as Lord and as witness to the universal love of God. It would necessitate some account of revelation in direct conflict with the general understanding of how religious knowledge is arrived at which I have been putting forward. At the heart of any such alternative account would have to stand an interpretation of the incarnation, which stressed its discontinuity with all preceding forms of witness to God, and insisted on the exclusivity and finality of Jesus as the revelation of God. Rahner, as we have seen, tried valiantly, but in my view unsuccessfully, to combine that latter insistence with the idea of a universal divine offer of self-communication to humankind. An understanding of incarnation which emphasizes its discontinuity and exclusivity in relation to the wider religious history of the human race, can have no place in and leaves no place for a theology for dialogue.

To suggest the need for revision on the issue of incarnation is, of course, a much more substantial and controversial proposal than to insist on the universal approach of God to humankind being both creative and redemptive in character. One factor that has become increasingly evident as the result of discussion of this issue in recent years is the imprecision of such terms as 'uniqueness' and 'incarnation'. It is therefore important to be clear about what understanding of 'incarnation' may be in need of revision. Sarah Coakley, in her excellent discussion of Troeltsch's christology, has offered a careful delineation of six different senses in which the term is used. In defining the fifth of her six understandings of the term, she describes it as involving an

> explicit claim of *qualitative* uniqueness in Christ; that is, it understands the 'incarnation' to imply that no other person could ever be like this again, or convey God in this way. The 'incarnation' on this fifth view means that Christ is in a category distinct from all other forms of revelation; the divine manifestation in him is thus both exclusive and final; it is qualitatively superior to all others, and it can never be sur-passed.[7]

It is this sense of incarnation that Rahner tried to hold on to, and that in my view cannot be fitted into a theology which would allow for open dialogue with other religions. Coakley's own assessment of the issue points in the same direction. She goes on to describe Troeltsch's discussion of the truth claims of the great world religions as having 'highlighted one of the most pressing difficulties (if not the most pressing difficulty) for any future "incarnational Christology" in this (our fifth) sense'.[8] And she returns to the point in her concluding discussion of the legacy of Troeltsch's christology where she speaks of

> its perception of the profound difficulties of maintaining a traditional 'incarnational' Christology in the face of certain cumulative aporias of modern theology: historical criticism,

historical relativism, the so-called 'other' world religions, an expanding universe, and so on.[9]

Once again the implication is clear that any proposal for revision at this point will not be an *ad hoc* proposal simply designed to accommodate the truth claims of other religions. Even if that is, in her judgment, the most pressing difficulty, it is only one of a cumulative series of difficulties pointing in the same direction.

But what also emerges from her careful analysis of Troeltsch's christology is that revision at this point does not automatically carry with it all the corollaries that it is often assumed to entail. Three points need to be emphasised. In the first place it does not necessarily involve the abandonment of an incarnational christology altogether. Coakley's fourth understanding of incarnation affirms 'a total interaction of the divine and human in Christ', 'a complete self-gift of God in Jesus', 'such that one can talk of Jesus as being "fully God" as well as "fully man" '.[10] That is clearly an incarnational view, but it lacks the claim to be necessarily final and exclusive of any possibility of other incarnations.

It was a view of that kind that I see as emerging more naturally from the overall character of Rahner's theology. It has, as I have pointed out already, its own difficulties in terms of how it is to be substantiated as a historical reality, and not just as an ideal concept. It is not part of my present purpose to assess whether or not those difficulties can be overcome. The significant point for the immediate discussion is that it does not carry the same negative implication for dialogue with other religions that Coakley's fifth sense does. It is a view, therefore, that can perfectly well have a place within a Christian theology for dialogue of the kind that I am trying to set out. There is no inherent contradiction between holding it and entering into a fully open dialogue with adherents of other faiths.

Secondly the kind of revision I am calling for does not necessitate the denial of religious significance to the historical figure of Jesus of Nazareth.[11] Here, again, there are serious difficulties, arising from historical critical method, about how that religious significance can function in a genuinely historical way. But those difficulties impinge equally on all Christians who give significance to the historical figure of Jesus, whatever their understanding of incarnation. Inter-religious dialogue does not necessitate a faith which is concerned only with ideas and not at all with the actualities of history, past or present.

Finally the proposed line of revision does not undermine the absoluteness of the Christian's faith commitment. This is the point at which the most serious reservations are likely to be felt. For it is to Christ that that commitment is made in Christian faith, and it is precisely the finality of Christ that is being called into question. Yet commitment to Christ is never to Christ alone. It is offered, like Christian prayer, to God the Father through Jesus Christ. The same point can be made by insisting that commitment to Christ is intimately linked with belief in the Holy Spirit. 'Christ', says D'Costa, 'is both the norm for understanding God and yet not a static one, but one that is constantly being transformed and enriched through the guiding/ declaring/judging function of the Spirit.'[12] Christ, that is to say, is the central symbol of a faith, which focusses on the historical figure of Jesus, but which draws on a more wide-ranging history, extending both before and after the time of Jesus, for its understanding of him. The figure of Christ has undergone many changes in the course of Christian history. And there are major differences today between, for example, the Christ of the liberation theologians and the base communities of South America on the one hand, and the Christ celebrated in an Eastern Orthodox liturgy on the other. Some of the changes in the way Christ is apprehended have arisen from renewed attention to the history of Jesus. But not all. They have been the result of many influences from many different sources. The absoluteness of the Christian's commitment is always to the mysterious God, made known to us in the face of Jesus Christ. But the contours of that face are not uniform or unchanging to human eyes. So on any understanding of Jesus, however strongly incarnational, the absolute commitment can never be to Christ as we know him. A revised understanding of incarnation will not alter that fact. Christ can still serve as the symbol of our full commitment, which is offered through him to God. The value of that formulation is that it recognizes the two vital characteristics of Christian commitment. The commitment is not empty. It is to a Christ whom we know primarily through Jesus but also through the varied history of Christian experience down the ages. And that gives to our commitment a specificity of content. But it has also to be remembered that that content has contained, and still does contain, seriously conflicting features between the different ways in which it has been expressed. These have been sufficient to give grounds for people to speak on occasion of incompatible Christianities, in much the same way as they more readily speak of incompatible religions. Absoluteness of commitment to a one-sided or distorted apprehension of Christ is fraught with danger. The absoluteness of commitment is to Christ as symbol of the God who is ultimate mystery. Christ, like the human conscience, can only rightly claim an absoluteness of commitment, if that commitment includes as an integral part of it an openness to the correction of its content as we now conceive it.

Any revision to the central doctrine of christology is bound to have repercussions on other aspects of Christian doctrine. It will bear particularly on theologies of atonement and of the church, whose close links with christology are witnessed by their familiar descriptions as the work of Christ and the body of Christ. The kind of modification that is called for is commensurate with that already proposed in relation to christology, and I can therefore indicate its general direction quite briefly. Accounts of the atonement and of the church speak of a divine forgiveness and of a divine community that spring historically from the fact of Jesus and also derive their power more fundamentally from the person of Christ. That basic character of the two doctrines is unaffected by the needs of a theology that will be open to inter-religious dialogue. What is affected are the claims to finality and exclusiveness, parallel to and dependent on the similar claims in relation to the person of Christ, that have frequently been seen as a part of their essential character. What must be expunged from our theology is the necessity to salvation of a conscious response to the sacrificial death of Christ or of entry into membership of the institutional church. We saw earlier something of the form the latter claim has taken in the past, with its epigrammatic summation in the words 'no salvation outside the church'.[13]

In the case of these two doctrines, there has already been a widespread movement of thought in the direction that I am proposing. What I want to stress for our immediate purpose is that the implications of that movement of thought are, as in the case of christology, relatively restricted. They do not undermine the reality or importance of the concept of atonement or of ecclesiology as such. Nor

75

do they abolish the significance of the historical fact of Christ's death or the historical emergence of the church as a result of his life, death and resurrection. Nor again do they retract from the reality of divine forgiveness or of divine presence apprehended through the cross and in the church. What they do stress is the relatively traditional insistence that both cross and church are particular historical manifestations of an eternal love of God, in which the ideals of compassionate forgiveness and communal existence are permanent realities. The earthly cross and the historical church are pointers to cross and to community at the heart of God. In the vivid imagery of two very early Christian writers there was 'a Lamb slain before the foundation of the world' and there was a 'church . . . that was created as the first of all things'.[14] Calvary and the institutional church are not necessarily their only instantiations in history.

My discussion of the doctrines of atonement and of the church so far has reflected on them as the grounds of divine forgiveness and of life-giving community as experienced by Christians. But those themes do not exhaust their significance. The universality of the Christ whose cross and whose body are the substance of those doctrines speaks also of a gospel to be proclaimed and a mission to be carried out. Does a questioning of their finality undermine the whole conception of a Christian gospel and a Christian mission? It certainly modifies the way in which they have often been understood. As John Macquarrie has said:

There must be an end to the imperialistic dream of a single religion for all the peoples of the earth. This does not, I think, mean an end to mission, but it does mean that the conception of mission needs to be continually rethought.[15]

The mission of proclaiming the gospel cannot be seen as the presentation to people of the only path to salvation, something previously unavailable to them. But the true heart of mission is to share with others the goodness of God made known in Jesus Christ. That possibility and that motive remain unaltered. And if the underlying account that I have been putting forward of God's self-giving to the world and the positive significance of other religious traditions as (like the Christian) partial and imperfect responses to it built up over many centuries has any validity, then there is no other way in which such sharing can be done with integrity than through a process of mutually receptive dialogue. So, far from eliminating a theology of mission, a theology for dialogue clarifies the form that it needs to take. It is no coincidence that missionaries have figured among those who have made a major contribution towards the initiation of inter-religious dialogue.

The account I have been offering of a theology *for* dialogue can be seen from one angle to call for a radical revision of traditional theologies. Its perspectival, parabolic and provisional character cuts out the possibility of claims to finality or exclusiveness of revealed truth. But that fact, I have gone on to argue, does not entail as radical a revision of the central doctrines affected as is often assumed to be the case. There may be other pressures, arising out of historical, moral or sociological considerations, which are pointing to the need for still further revision, but those are not my immediate concern. And it can hardly be doubted that a theology *of* dialogue, a theology arising out of the experience of dialogue with one or more of the other major religions, will raise new possibilities and new necessities of further revision. While it would be in general premature, and for me personally impossible, to forecast the substance of any such further revision that might be called for, something does need to be said about the general way in which a Christian theology might expect to change in the light of such dialogue.

The pluralism of theologies within Christianity, to which we have grown increasingly accustomed, may provide us with an appropriate model. Liberation theology or feminist theology takes a dominant contemporary concern and sets about reinterpreting Christian theology as a whole with that concern, and the symbols through which it finds expression, as its determining interpretative categories. Extreme exponents of such theologies sometimes claim that their particular form of Christian theology constitutes the only valid one. More often the claim takes the more modest and more plausible form of asserting that it is a way of highlighting a much needed and hitherto neglected characteristic of Christian theology. It will then be seen as one form of Christian theology alongside others, but one which has a particularly important role to fulfil at the present time and from which all other theologies need to learn and to draw. Sometimes that learning will be simply a matter of recapturing elements in Christian thought that have been relatively neglected or down played. At other times it will involve the correction of beliefs that from the new perspective come to be seen as seriously distorted or in error. The history of Christianity's earlier relation with another religious tradition, the philosophico-religious Platonism of the early centuries of the Christian era, which I referred to in the first chapter,[16] reinforces the suitability of this model for our present concern. What happened in that case was the emergence of Platonic forms of Christian theology, in which the insights of a religious Platonism played a co-ordinating role in ordering the insights of Christian history and Christian symbolism. We might look forward in a similar way to the emergence of Islamic or Buddhistic forms of Christian theology. These would take insights emerging from the dialogue with the other religion and use them in a similar way to provide a new ordering of Christian resources. They would stand as particular forms of Christian theology alongside others, but would also have implications for those other theologies, sometimes calling for the bringing to the fore of relatively submerged elements within them and at other times calling for the correction of old beliefs now seen to be no longer worthy of assent.

The ultimate goal of such a process is too far beyond the horizon even for conjecture. But the radical differences and points of conflicts between the major world religions render the notion of a single unified world theology hard to conceive. Moreover the richness of the varieties of human experience and the vitality inherent in the particularities of differing religious symbolisms make the prospect uncalled for and unexciting. The comparison of it to a form of 'Ecumenical Esperanto', though intended by one writer as an argument in its favour,[17] is more widely and more wisely seen as a disincentive to any such aspiration.[18] 'A single world religion is', in John Hick's words 'not a consummation to be desired.'[19]

So it is explicitly Christian theology, expressive of Christian faith, with which we are and will continue to be concerned. It is a Christian theology chastened by being forced to recognize more radically than it has normally been prepared to do the contingency of its history, its symbols and its understanding. But it does not, I have been arguing, reflect a Christianity robbed of the absoluteness of commitment that is proper to a full religious faith. The finality which Christians have traditionally ascribed to the person of Christ is an expression of the conviction

79

that in Christ Christians are truly directed and joined to the ultimate reality of the being and the love of God. But the relation of *that* finality (the fact that in Christ Christians are united to that which is ultimate and final in the world, which we name God) to those things to which other religions ascribe finality or ultimacy (what John Taylor in the passage I quoted earlier called the 'jealousies' of other faiths[20]) remains an open question. There is no possibility of determining that question until we have entered with the fullest degree of empathy into dialogue with those other faiths and travelled quite a long way down that road. There is, Christians have always acknowledged, a finality that belongs to the eschaton, to the final goal of history, which transcends any anticipation of it that we may experience in the present.

I began by stressing the limited role that the theologian may be called on to play within the process of inter-religious dialogue as a whole. My immediate concern has been with the feasibility of a theology in terms of which a Christian might be able to justify his or her own partici-pation as a committed Christian in genuinely open dia-logue. But dialogue involves two participants. The only requirements that one participant can make of his or her partner in dialogue are requirements imposed by the nature of dialogue as such. One of the things that I have been emphasizing as a vital feature of a Christian theology for dialogue seems to me to belong to that category and therefore to be of wider application than just the prelimi-nary stage that has been my concern; and that is a revision-ary approach to one's own religious faith and practice. That is something which, as I have pointed out, no religion finds easy to accommodate. It is in *prima facie* conflict with the absoluteness of commitment generally character-istic of religious claims. Christians have not, and still do not find it easy to accept, despite the fact that there are facets of Christianity and of Christian history which are congenial to such an attitude. For some other religions the adoption of such an approach has even greater obstacles to overcome. Yet there are signs that this is not a forlorn hope, even in the case of Islam where the difficulties to be overcome might seem to be particularly great. Fazlur Rahman, for example, speaks of the Qur'an's 'strong rejection of exclusivism and election'.[21] And Mohamed Talbi argues the case in a way very similar to that which I have adopted. He writes:

> With very few exceptions the theological systems of all religious confessions have been based on the axiom, expressed in different ways, that 'outside the Church there is no salvation' . . . This leads to the conclusion that apart from certain chosen ones, the majority of human beings are destined for perdition. And yet all faiths proclaim that God is Justice, Mercy and Love! It is precisely in this area that we need a real theological renewal and a radical change of mentality.[22]

And he goes on to claim that examples of the approach he is advocating are already to be found in some mainstream orthodox Islamic theologians in earlier centuries.[23] No doubt his view is a minority one in contemporary Islam. But the parallel view that I am advocating is also a minority one (if not so small a minority) within contemporary Christianity. We are not talking about a process where we can or should be looking for quick results. But there is certainly nothing more important for all the religions of the world than a recognition that full commitment and openness to change are not incompatible, that loyalty and self-criticism can coexist; indeed, that the former implies the latter in each case. The menace of unself-critical religion is all around us. A patient but persistent pleading for such an approach within the Christian sphere is the essential first step in developing a theology for dialogue. It is likely to prove the essential first step also in the dialogue itself.

Notes

Preface

1 'Christianity and Other Faiths', *Theology* XCI, July 1988, pp.302–8.

1 The Precedents of the Past

1 J. Taylor, 'The Theological Basis of Interfaith Dialogue' in J. Hick and B. Hebblethwaite (ed.), *Christianity and Other Religions*, Collins 1980, pp.212–33.

2 M. Barnes, *Religions in Conversation*, SPCK 1989, p.89.

3 W. Cantwell Smith, 'The Christian in a Religiously plural World' in J. Hick and B. Hebblethwaite (ed.), op. cit., p.100.

4 G. Parrinder, 'The Salvation of other men' in E.J. Sharpe and J.R. Hinnels (ed.), *Man and His Salvation*, Manchester University Press 1973, p.196.

5 J. Macquarrie, 'Christianity and Other Faiths', *Union Seminary Quarterly Review* 20, November 1964, p.39.

6 J.A.T. Robinson, *Truth is Two-Eyed*, SCM Press 1979, p.105; K. Stendahl, 'Notes for Three Bible Studies' in G.H. Anderson and T.F. Stransky (ed.), *Christ's Lordship and Religious Pluralism*, Orbis 1981, pp.12–15; Paul F. Knitter, *No Other Name?*, Orbis and SCM Press 1985, p.185.

7 J. Cobb, 'Dialogue' in L. Swidler, J. Cobb, Paul Knitter, Monika Hellwig, *Death or Dialogue?*, SCM Press and Trinity Press International 1990, pp.16–18; J. Macquarrie, *Jesus Christ in Modern Thought*, SCM Press and Trinity Press International 1990, p.422.

8 See e.g. G.W.H. Lampe, *God as Spirit*, Oxford University Press 1977, p.31; J. Cobb, ibid.

9 Denzinger, *Enchiridion* 1351.

10 Luther, *Larger Catechism* II 3.

11 E.F. Jacob, 'Nicholas of Cusa' in F.J.C. Hearnshaw (ed.), *The Social and Political Ideas of Some Great Thinkers of the Renaissance and the Reformation*, London 1925, pp.53–7.

12 J.J. Lipner, 'Does Copernicus Help?', *Religious Studies* 13, June 1977, pp.250–1; J. Maritain, *Redeeming the Time*, Geoffrey Bles 1943, pp.105f.

13 R. Panikkar, *The Unknown Christ of Hinduism*, Darton Longman & Todd, rev ed. 1981, p.18.

14 H. Küng, *On Being a Christian*, Collins 1977, pp.97–8.

15 Paul F. Knitter, *No Other Name?*, pp.123–4.

16 John Hick, 'The Copernican Revolution in Theology' in *God and the Universe of Faiths*, Macmillan 1973, pp.121–2.

17 J.J. Lipner, art. cit., p.249.

18 John Hick, *art. cit.*, pp.123–6. 'Repeal' is John Hick's own word ('The Non-Absoluteness of Christianity' in ed. John Hick and Paul F. Knitter (ed.), *The Myth of Christian Uniqueness*, SCM Press and Orbis 1987, p.20).

19 Augustine, *Enchiridion* 27, 103. Cf. also Augustine, *On Rebuke and Grace* 14,44; Aquinas, *Summa Theologiae* 1.19.6 ad 1; Bucer, *Commentary on Romans*, 9.17; Calvin, *Commentary on I Timothy*, 2.4.

20 Karl Rahner, 'Christianity and the non-Christian Religions', *Theological Investigations* 5, Darton, Longman & Todd 1966, p.122.

21 Arnold Toynbee, *Christianity Among the Religions of the Word*, Oxford University Press 1958, p.110.

2 The Pressures of the Present

1 K. Ward, *The Living God*, SPCK 1984, Ch.8, especially p.97. Keith Ward has developed these ideas more fully in relation to some of those other great religious traditions in his later book, *Images of Eternity*, Darton, Longman & Todd 1987.

2 Hugo Meynell, 'Towards a New Dialectic of Religions', *Religious Studies* 18, December 1982, p.424.

3 J. Macquarrie, art. cit., p.43, citing E. Brunner *The Mediator*, Macmillan 1934, p.201.
4 E. Brunner, *Revelation and Reason*, SCM Press 1947, p.258.
5 H. Kraemer, *Why Christianity of all Religions?*, Lutterworth 1962, p.95 n.1.
6 K. Barth, *Church Dogmatics* 1/2, T & T Clark 1956, pp.297–338, esp. pp.298 and 327.
7 H. Kraemer, op. cit., p.15 and p.95 n.1 (italics and capitals original).
8 J.V. Taylor, art. cit., pp.224–6
9 Ibid., p.232
10 J. Macquarrie, art. cit., p.40
11 I have developed this approach to religious language more fully in my *Faith and the Mystery of God* SCM Press 1982, ch.2.
12 Nicholas of Cusa, *De Docta Ignorantia* I:2.
13 F.F. Jacob, 'Cusanus the Theologian', *Bulletin of the John Rylands Library* 21.2, October 1937, p.409.
14 Nicholas of Cusa, op. cit., I:3.
15 G.A. Lindbeck, *The Nature of Doctrine*, SPCK 1984.
16 Richard B. Miller, 'The Reference of "God" ', *Faith and Philosophy* 3, 1986, pp.1–14, esp. p.14 (italics original). My example of the different groups of hunters is a development of one used by Miller in the article.
17 See Barnes, op. cit., p.127.
18 Roger Trigg, 'Religion and the Threat of Relativism', *Religious Studies* 19, 1983, p.310.
19 Jürgen Moltmann, 'Is "Pluralistic Theology" Useful for the Dialogue of World Religions?' in Gavin d'Costa (ed.), *The Myth of a Pluralistic Theology of Religions*, Orbis 1990, p.155.

3   A Test Case: The Theology of Karl Rahner

1 This paragraph includes material also to be found in my article 'Can theology still be about God?' in S. Davaney (ed.), *Theology at the End of Modernity*, Trinity Press International 1991, pp.221–32.
2 K. Rahner, 'On the Importance of the Non-Christian Religions for Salvation', *Theological Investigations* 18, Darton, Longman & Todd 1984, pp.293–5 (italics original).

3 'Jesus Christ in the non-Christian Religions', *Theological Investigations* 17, 1981, pp.41–2.

4 'Christology within an Evolutionary View of the World', *Theological Investigations* 5, 1966, p.160 (= *Foundations of Christian Faith*, Darton, Longman & Todd 1978, p.181).

5 'Jesus Christ in the non-Christian Religions; *Theological Investigations* 17, p.46.

6 See p.14 above.

7 John Robertson Jr, 'Rahner and Odgen: Man's Knowledge of God', *Harvard Theological Review* 63.3, July 1970, p.401.

8 K. Rahner, 'Nature and Grace', *Theological Investigations* 4, 1966, p.183. Cf. also 'Concerning the Relationship between Nature and Grace', *Theological Investigations* 1, 1961, pp.313–15.

9 See e.g. G. Vass, *The Mystery of Man and the Foundations of a Theological System*, Sheed and Ward 1985, Vol. 2, p.71 (also citing Von Balthasar to similar effect); M. Taylor, *God is Love*, Scholars Press 1986, pp.145–6.

10 'Experience of Transcendence form the Standpoint of Catholic Dogmatics', *Theological Investigations* 18, pp.181.

11 A. Gerken, *Offenbarung und Transzendenzerfahrung*, Dusseldorf 1969, p.35, cited by M. Taylor, op. cit., p.198.

12 B. Marshall, *Christology in Conflict*, Blackwell 1987, p.106.

13 *Theological Investigations* 5, pp.157–192 (Very largely reproduced under the same title as Ch.vi.1 of *Foundations of Christian Faith* pp.178–203).

14 Art. cit. p.158 (=*Foundations of Christian Faith* p.179).

15 K. Rahner, *Foundations of Christian Faith*, pp.249–50.

16 'Christology within an Evolutionary View of the World', *Theological Investigations* 5, p.198.

17 J. Macquarrie, *Principles of Christian Theology*, 2nd ed. SCM Press and Charles Scribner 1977, p.172.

18 K. Rahner, 'Christology within an Evolutionary View of the World', *Theological Investigations* 5, p.188 (italics original).

19 Ibid., p.160 (=*Foundation of Christian Faith*, p. 181).

Notes

4 A Theology for Dialogue

1 R. Swinburne, *Faith and Reason*, Clarendon Press 1981, p.177.
2 K. Ward, *Divine Action*, Collins 1990, p.230.
3 Christoph Schwöbel, 'Particularity, Universality and the Religions' in G. D'Costa (ed.), *Christian Uniqueness Reconsidered*, Orbis 1990, p.43 (italics added).
4 See Chapter 1 n. 19. At that point I was concerned only with Augustine's interpretation of I Tim. 2.4 as meaning simply that all who are saved are saved in accordance with God's will. The passage cited (*Enchiridion* 27, 103) also goes on to interpret John 1.9 in a similar fashion as meaning simply that all who are enlightened are enlightened by God.
5 See pp.27–30 above.
6 L. Newbigin 'The Centrality of Jesus for History' in M. Goulder (ed.), *Incarnation and Myth*, SCM Press 1979, p.208. Newbigin's position summarized here is spelt out more fully in an earlier book, *The Finality of Christ*, SCM Press 1969.
7 Sarah Coakley, *Christ Without Absolutes*, Oxford University Press 1988, pp.105–6.
8 Ibid., p.115.
9 Ibid., p.191.
10 Ibid., p.105.
11 See Coakley, op. cit., pp.155–63 for defense of Troeltsch's concern with the historian's Jesus.
12 Gavin D'Costa 'Christ, the Trinity, and Religious Plurality' in G. D'Costa (ed.), op.cit., p.23.
13 See pp.11–12 above.
14 Rev. 13.8; Shepherd of Hermas, *Visions* 4.2 (Cf. also II Clement 14.2).
15 J. Macquarrie, art. cit., pp.44–5.
16 See pp.16–17 above.
17 See L.J. Swidler, 'Interreligious and Interideological Dialogue' in L.J. Swidler (ed.), *Towards a Universal Theology of Religion*, Orbis 1987, pp.20ff.
18 See J. Macquarrie. art. cit., pp.45–6.
19 J. Hick, 'Whatever Path Men Choose is Mine' in Hick and Hebblethwaite (ed.) *Christianity and Other Religions*, p.189.
20 See pp.31–2 above.

87

21 Fazlur Rahman 'The People of the Book and the Diversity of "Religions" ', in Paul J. Griffiths (ed.), *Christianity Through Non-Christian Eyes*, Orbis 1990, p.106.
22 Mohamed Talbi 'Islam and Dialogue – Some Reflections on a Current Topic' in Griffiths (ed.), op. cit, pp.91–2.
23 Ibid., pp.92–3.

Index

Index